Michele Nalley

The Real Estate Investors Blueprint
Essential Steps for Acquiring, Managing, and Profiting from Rental Properties

Michele D. Nalley MS, NAR
American Real Estate Executive, Entrepreneur and Author

Michele Nalley

Copyright © 2024
All Rights Reserved
ISBN: 9798332884955

Michele Nalley

Acknowledgment

Writing The Real Estate Investor's Blueprint: Essential Steps for Acquiring, Managing, and Profiting from Rental Properties has been a deeply rewarding journey, one that would not have been possible without the unwavering support and inspiration from those closest to me.

First and foremost, I want to express my heartfelt gratitude to my children, Keyla Nalley and Brandon Nalley. Your constant encouragement, understanding, and love have been my driving force. Keyla, your resilience and determination inspire me every day. Brandon, your curiosity and enthusiasm for learning remind me of the importance of continuous growth and improvement. Both of you have been my greatest cheerleaders and have provided me with the motivation to pursue my dreams and share my knowledge through this book.

To Keyla and Brandon, thank you for believing in me and for being my pillars of strength. Your patience and support have been invaluable, especially during the late nights and long hours dedicated to writing this book. Your presence in my life has made this accomplishment all the more meaningful.

I would also like to extend my gratitude to the entire team at MKB Investment. Your hard work and dedication have been instrumental in the success of our real estate ventures and have provided a solid foundation for the insights shared in this book. To my colleagues and mentors at Inner Circle Capital, Black Briar Advisors, and The Orlando Housing Authority, thank you for the opportunities and experiences that have shaped my career and enriched my understanding of the real estate industry.

Finally, to my readers, thank you for embarking on this journey with me. I hope this book serves as a valuable resource in your real estate investment endeavors and that it helps you achieve your financial goals and dreams.

With deepest appreciation,

Michele Nalley

About the Author

Michele Nalley is an accomplished American real estate executive, entrepreneur, author, and the visionary founder and CEO of MKB Investment. With over 30 years of extensive experience in the real estate industry, Michele has held executive positions at some of the most prestigious real estate companies, including Inner Circle Capital, Black Briar Advisors, and The Orlando Housing Authority.

Michele's educational background is as impressive as her professional achievements. She holds a Bachelor of Science degree from the University of Central Florida and a Master's degree in Real Estate from Florida International University. Additionally, Michele is a licensed real estate professional in the state of Florida, further solidifying her expertise and commitment to the field.

As the Founder and CEO of MKB Investment, Michele has built and continues to manage a thriving real estate empire. Her company specializes in acquiring, managing, and profiting from rental properties, showcasing her adeptness in both strategic planning and hands-on property management.

In her book, The Real Estate Investor's Blueprint: Essential Steps for Acquiring, Managing, and Profiting from Rental Properties, Michele shares her wealth of knowledge and experience, providing invaluable insights and practical steps for both novice and seasoned investors. Her dedication to empowering others in the real estate industry shines through in her detailed guidance, making this book an essential resource for anyone looking to achieve success in property investment.

Preface

Welcome to The Real Estate Investor's Blueprint: Essential Steps for Acquiring, Managing, and Profiting from Rental Properties. Whether you are a novice investor just beginning your journey or a seasoned professional looking to sharpen your skills, this book is designed to provide you with the knowledge, tools, and strategies necessary to succeed in the dynamic world of real estate investing.

My journey in real estate began over three decades ago. With a Bachelor of Science degree from the University of Central Florida and a Master's degree in Real Estate from Florida International University, I embarked on a career that has taken me through various executive roles at some of the most esteemed real estate companies, including Inner Circle Capital, Black Briar Advisors, and The Orlando Housing Authority. These experiences have given me a deep understanding of the complexities and opportunities within the real estate market.

In 2005, I founded MKB Investment with a vision to build a robust portfolio of rental properties and help others achieve financial independence through real estate. Today, I am proud to manage a thriving real estate empire that continues to grow and adapt to market changes. The journey has been challenging but incredibly rewarding, and it is my passion for real estate and a desire to share my knowledge that has led to the creation of this book.

The Real Estate Investor's Blueprint is structured to

guide you through every step of the real estate investment process. From understanding market trends and securing financing to managing properties and planning for long-term success, each chapter is packed with practical advice and actionable insights. I have drawn on my extensive experience to provide real-world examples and proven strategies that you can apply to your own investments.

This book is not just about acquiring properties; it is about building a sustainable and profitable real estate business. You will learn how to set clear investment goals, develop a strategic plan, and execute it with confidence. You will also discover the importance of risk management, financial planning, and continuous learning in achieving long-term success.

Real estate investing is a journey, and like any journey, it requires preparation, perseverance, and a willingness to learn and adapt. I hope this book serves as a valuable roadmap for your journey, helping you navigate the challenges and seize the opportunities that come your way.

Thank you for choosing The Real Estate Investor's Blueprint. I am excited to share this knowledge with you and look forward to seeing you succeed in your real estate endeavors.

Sincerely,

Michele Nalley

Michele Nalley

Contents

Acknowledgment: ii
About the Author: iii
Preface: iv

Chapter 1: Introduction

Chapter 2: Getting Started in Real Estate Investing

Chapter 3: Financial Planning and Budgeting

Chapter 4: Finding the Right Properties

Chapter 5: Acquisitions and Closings

Chapter 6: Renovations and Property Improvements

Chapter 7: Renting Out Your Properties

Chapter 8: Property Management

Chapter 9: Scaling Your Portfolio

Chapter 10: Navigating Challenges

Chapter 11: Long-term Success and Exit Strategies

Michele Nalley

Page Left Blank Intentionally

Chapter 1

Introduction

Embarking on a journey in real estate investment begins with a deep understanding of the real estate market. This foundational knowledge is crucial for making informed decisions, identifying lucrative opportunities, and mitigating potential risks. In this section, we will explore the critical aspects of understanding the real estate market, including market dynamics, research and analysis, key market indicators, market cycles, and leveraging local knowledge.

Understanding Market Dynamics

Real estate market dynamics are influenced by various factors that affect supply and demand, property values, and rental rates. Key factors include economic conditions, population growth, employment rates, and interest rates. Each of these factors plays a significant role in shaping the real estate landscape.

- Economic Conditions: The overall economic health of a region significantly impacts the real estate market. A robust economy with high employment rates and rising incomes typically leads to increased demand for housing. Conversely, economic downturns can result in decreased demand and falling property values. Investors must keep an eye on economic indicators such as GDP growth, unemployment rates, and consumer confidence to gauge the market's health.

- Population Growth: Areas experiencing population growth often see increased demand for housing. This demand can drive property values and rental rates higher. Investors should look for regions with positive population growth trends, which can indicate a healthy and growing real estate market.

- Employment Rates: Employment rates directly influence people's ability to rent or purchase homes. High employment rates generally lead to higher demand for housing, while high unemployment rates can reduce demand. Investors should focus on areas with strong job markets and diverse employment opportunities to ensure a steady demand for rental properties.

- Interest Rates: Interest rates affect the cost of borrowing money to finance real estate investments. Lower interest rates make borrowing cheaper, encouraging more investment and increasing demand for properties. Conversely, higher interest rates can dampen demand. Keeping an eye on interest rate trends and monetary policies is essential for investors to make informed financing decisions.
- Research and Analysis

Thorough research and analysis are fundamental to

understanding the real estate market and identifying promising investment opportunities. Here are some essential steps to conduct effective market research:

- Market Segmentation: Real estate markets are not homogenous; they consist of various segments such as residential, commercial, industrial, and mixed-use properties. Investors should identify which market segment aligns with their investment goals and expertise.

- Local Economic Indicators: Analyze local economic indicators such as median household income, job growth, and population trends. These indicators provide insights into the economic health and potential demand for housing in a specific area.

- Supply and Demand Analysis: Examine the supply and demand dynamics in the target market. High demand and limited supply can drive property values and rental rates up. Conversely, oversupply can lead to price stagnation or decline. Tools like vacancy rates, absorption rates, and new construction permits can help gauge supply and demand.

- Comparative Market Analysis (CMA): Conducting a CMA involves comparing similar properties in the target area to determine their market value. This analysis helps investors set competitive rental rates and identify properties priced below market value.

- Online Resources and Tools: Leverage online

resources, such as real estate websites, market reports, and industry databases, to gather data and insights. Websites like Zillow, Realtor.com, and Redfin provide valuable information on property values, rental rates, and market trends.

Identifying Key Market Indicators

Key market indicators provide valuable insights into the health and potential of a real estate market. Monitoring these indicators can help investors make informed decisions and identify emerging opportunities. Here are some critical market indicators to consider:

- Median Home Prices: The median home price is a crucial indicator of property value trends in a specific market. Rising median home prices suggest increasing demand and potential appreciation, while declining prices may indicate a slowing market.

- Rental Rates: Rental rates reflect the income potential of rental properties. Analyze rental rate trends to determine whether the market is favorable for landlords. High rental rates relative to property values can indicate strong rental demand and profitability.

- Days on Market (DOM): DOM measures the average time it takes for properties to sell. A low DOM indicates a hot market with high demand, while a high DOM suggests a slower market. Investors should look for markets with a low DOM for quicker turnover.

- Inventory Levels: Inventory levels represent the number of available properties for sale or rent. Low inventory levels indicate high demand and potential for price appreciation, while high inventory levels can signal oversupply and price stagnation.

- Vacancy Rates: Vacancy rates measure the percentage of unoccupied rental properties. Low vacancy rates indicate strong rental demand and stability, while high vacancy rates suggest a struggling rental market. Aim for markets with low vacancy rates to ensure consistent rental income.

- Cap Rates: Capitalization rates (cap rates) measure the potential return on investment for rental properties. A higher cap rate indicates a higher potential return but may also involve higher risk. Investors should balance cap rates with market stability and growth potential.

Understanding Market Cycles

Real estate markets are cyclical, characterized by periods of expansion, stability, and contraction. Understanding market cycles is crucial for timing investments and maximizing returns. Here are the key phases of real estate market cycles:

- Expansion Phase: During the expansion phase, the market experiences rising property values, increased construction activity, and strong demand for housing. This phase is ideal for acquiring properties as they appreciate in value. Investors should focus on identifying emerging markets and properties with growth potential.

- Stability Phase: The stability phase is characterized by moderate price increases and balanced supply and demand. The market is neither booming nor declining significantly. This phase offers steady rental income and minimal risk. Investors should focus on maintaining and managing their existing properties while preparing for potential market shifts.

- Contraction Phase: The contraction phase occurs when the market experiences declining property values, decreased construction activity, and reduced demand for housing. This phase can present opportunities to acquire properties at discounted prices. Investors should be cautious and focus on properties with strong fundamentals and potential for long-term appreciation.

Understanding market cycles allows investors to align their strategies with the current phase. During expansion phases, focus on acquiring properties and leveraging growth. In stability phases, prioritize cash flow and property management. During contraction phases, seek undervalued properties and prepare for the next expansion.

Leveraging Local Knowledge

Local knowledge and expertise play a vital role in successful real estate investing. Engaging with local professionals and leveraging their insights can provide a competitive edge. Here are some ways to leverage local knowledge:

- Real Estate Agents and Brokers: Local real estate agents and brokers have in-depth knowledge of the market and can provide valuable insights into property values, rental rates, and neighborhood trends. They can also help identify off-market deals and negotiate favorable terms.

- Property Managers: Property managers have hands-on experience with rental properties in the area. They can provide insights into tenant preferences, rental demand, and property maintenance. Partnering with a reliable property manager can enhance property performance and tenant satisfaction.

- Local Investors and Networking: Joining local real estate investment groups and networking with experienced investors can provide valuable insights and opportunities. Local investors often share their experiences, market trends, and potential investment deals.

- Municipal Resources: Local government and municipal resources, such as planning departments and economic development agencies, can provide information on upcoming infrastructure projects, zoning changes, and economic initiatives. These factors can significantly impact property values and investment potential.

- Community Involvement: Getting involved in the local community and attending neighborhood meetings can provide firsthand insights into the area's dynamics and future developments. Building relationships with community members can also help identify emerging opportunities and potential challenges.

Understanding the real estate market is the foundation of a successful investment journey. By comprehending market dynamics, conducting thorough research and analysis, monitoring key market indicators, understanding market cycles, and leveraging local knowledge, investors can make informed decisions and capitalize on lucrative opportunities. Real estate markets are ever-evolving, so staying updated with the latest trends and continuously expanding your knowledge is essential for long-term success. With a solid understanding of the real estate market, investors can navigate the complexities of real estate investing and build a profitable and resilient investment portfolio.

Setting Goals and Objectives: Defining Your Real Estate Vision

Embarking on a journey in real estate investing requires a clear vision and well-defined goals. Setting goals and objectives is crucial for maintaining focus, measuring progress, and ultimately achieving success. In this section, we will explore the importance of setting goals, the process of defining your real estate vision, creating SMART goals, breaking down goals into milestones, and regularly reviewing and adjusting your goals.

Importance of Setting Goals

Setting goals provides clarity and direction, helping investors stay motivated and committed to their real estate journey. Here are some reasons why setting goals is essential:

- Clarity and Focus: Goals provide a clear sense of direction, helping investors focus their efforts on specific outcomes. This clarity prevents distractions and allows investors to allocate their resources effectively.

- Motivation and Commitment: Well-defined goals serve as a source of motivation, driving investors to stay committed to their investment strategy. Achieving milestones along the way provides a sense of accomplishment and reinforces the commitment to long-term objectives.

- Measurement and Accountability: Goals act as benchmarks for measuring progress and success. They enable investors to track their achievements, identify areas for improvement, and hold themselves accountable for their actions.

- Prioritization and Resource Allocation: Goals

help investors prioritize their actions and allocate resources efficiently. By focusing on high-impact activities that align with their goals, investors can maximize their chances of success.

- Adaptability and Flexibility: Setting goals allows investors to adapt and adjust their strategies based on changing market conditions and personal circumstances. Regularly reviewing and adjusting goals ensures that the investment plan remains relevant and achievable.

Defining Your Real Estate Vision

Defining your real estate vision involves envisioning your ideal future as a real estate investor. A clear vision provides a roadmap for your investment journey and guides your decision-making process.

Here are steps to help you define your real estate vision:

- Reflect on Long-term Aspirations: Start by reflecting on your long-term aspirations and what you hope to achieve through real estate investing. Consider factors such as financial independence, wealth accumulation, passive income generation, and personal fulfillment. Visualize the lifestyle you desire and the impact you want to create.

- Identify Core Values and Principles: Your real estate vision should align with your core values and principles. Identify what matters most to you, such as integrity, sustainability, community impact, or financial security. These values will serve as guiding principles for your investment decisions.

- Set a Time Horizon: Determine the time horizon for your real estate vision. Are you looking to achieve financial independence within five years, or are you focused on building a legacy for future generations? Setting a specific time frame helps you plan and prioritize your actions accordingly.

- Envision Your Ideal Portfolio: Imagine the composition of your ideal real estate portfolio. Consider the types of properties you want to invest in (residential, commercial, multifamily), the locations, and the scale of your portfolio. Visualize the income streams, property management structure, and overall impact of your portfolio.

- Consider Personal and Financial Goals: Your real estate vision should align with your personal and financial goals. Consider how real estate investing fits into your overall life plan. Do you want to supplement your income, achieve early retirement, or create a legacy for your family? Your vision should reflect your unique goals and aspirations.

Creating SMART Goals

To effectively achieve your real estate vision, it is

crucial to set SMART goals. SMART stands for Specific, Measurable, Achievable, Relevant, and Time-bound. Here's a breakdown of each component:

- Specific: Goals should be clear and well-defined. Avoid vague statements and focus on specific outcomes. For example, instead of saying, "I want to invest in real estate," specify, "I want to acquire three rental properties in the next two years."

- Measurable: Goals should have quantifiable criteria to track progress and evaluate success. Include specific metrics, such as the number of properties, rental income, or return on investment. Measurable goals enable you to assess your achievements objectively.

- Achievable: Goals should be realistic and attainable, considering your resources, capabilities, and market conditions. While it's important to set ambitious goals, ensure they are within your reach. Assess your financial situation, skills, and market opportunities to determine what is achievable.

- Relevant: Goals should align with your overall vision and contribute to your long-term objectives. Ensure that each goal is relevant to your real estate strategy and supports your broader aspirations. Avoid setting goals that do not align with your vision or distract you from your primary objectives.

- Time-bound: Goals should have a defined

timeframe, creating a sense of urgency and accountability. Set specific deadlines for achieving each goal. For example, instead of saying, "I want to increase my rental income," specify, "I want to increase my rental income by 20% within the next 12 months."

Breaking Down Goals into Milestones

Breaking down your long-term goals into smaller milestones makes them more manageable and achievable. Milestones represent significant progress points towards your ultimate vision. Here's how to break down your goals into actionable milestones:

- Identify Key Milestones: Start by identifying key milestones that mark significant progress towards your long-term goals. For example, if your goal is to acquire ten rental properties within five years, key milestones could include acquiring the first property within the first six months, acquiring three properties within two years, and so on.

- Set Specific Actions and Deadlines: For each milestone, define specific actions and deadlines. Break down the actions into smaller tasks that are manageable and achievable within the given timeframe. For example, if your milestone is to acquire the first property within six months, specific actions could include market research, securing financing, and making offers.

- Monitor Progress and Celebrate Achievements:

Regularly monitor your progress towards each milestone. Track your achievements and evaluate whether you are on track to meet your deadlines. Celebrate each milestone achieved, as it provides motivation and reinforces your commitment to the overall vision.

- Adjust and Adapt: Be flexible and open to adjusting your milestones if necessary. Real estate markets and personal circumstances can change, requiring you to adapt your approach. If you encounter unexpected challenges or opportunities, adjust your milestones and actions accordingly to stay on track towards your long-term goals.

Reviewing and Adjusting Goals

Regularly reviewing and adjusting your goals is essential to stay on track and adapt to changing circumstances. Here are steps to effectively review and adjust your goals:

- Set Regular Review Intervals: Establish regular intervals for reviewing your goals, such as quarterly or annually. Set aside dedicated time to evaluate your progress, assess the effectiveness of your strategies, and identify any obstacles or opportunities.

- Evaluate Progress and Performance: During each review, evaluate your progress towards your goals. Assess whether you are meeting your milestones and deadlines. Identify areas where you have excelled and areas that need improvement. Use this evaluation to make informed decisions about your next steps.

- Identify Obstacles and Challenges: Identify any obstacles or challenges that may be hindering your progress. Consider external factors such as market conditions, economic changes, or personal circumstances. Develop strategies to overcome these challenges and adjust your goals if necessary.

- Adjust Goals and Strategies: Based on your evaluation, adjust your goals and strategies as needed. If you have achieved certain goals ahead of schedule, consider setting more ambitious targets. If you are facing significant challenges, adjust your goals to be more realistic and attainable. Ensure that your goals remain aligned with your overall vision.

- Stay Committed and Flexible: Stay committed to your long-term vision, but be flexible in your approach. Real estate investing is a dynamic and evolving field, so adaptability is key. Continuously learn, seek feedback, and be willing to adjust your goals and strategies to navigate changing circumstances.

Setting goals and defining your real estate vision is a critical step in your investment journey. By understanding the importance of goals, creating a comprehensive vision, setting SMART goals, breaking them down into milestones, and regularly reviewing and adjusting your goals, you can stay focused, motivated, and on track to achieve long-term success.

Remember, your real estate vision is unique to you, so take the time to define it clearly and align your actions with your aspirations.

Financial Foundations: Basics of Real Estate Investing

Building a solid financial foundation is crucial for successful real estate investing. Understanding the basics of real estate finance, leveraging financing options, and managing your finances effectively are key components of a profitable investment strategy. In this section, we will explore the fundamental aspects of real estate finance, including understanding real estate financing, budgeting for investment, understanding cash flow, credit and financing strategies, and tax planning and strategies.

Understanding Real Estate Financing

Real estate financing involves securing the necessary funds to acquire and manage properties. There are various financing options available, each with its advantages and considerations. Understanding these options is essential for making informed financing decisions. Here are some common real estate financing options:

- Traditional Bank Loans: Traditional bank loans are one of the most common financing options for real estate investors. These loans typically offer lower interest rates and longer repayment terms. However, they may have stricter qualification requirements, including good credit scores, stable income, and a significant down payment.

- Private Lenders: Private lenders are individuals or companies that provide loans to real estate investors. These loans can be more flexible than traditional bank loans and may not require stringent credit checks. However, they often come with higher interest rates and shorter repayment terms.

- Hard Money Loans: Hard money loans are short-term loans secured by real estate. They are typically used for fix-and-flip projects or properties that require significant renovations. Hard money loans have higher interest rates and fees but offer quick approval and funding.

- Creative Financing Strategies: Creative financing strategies involve unconventional methods to acquire properties with limited upfront capital. Examples include seller financing, lease options, and partnerships. These strategies can be valuable for investors who want to leverage other people's resources to finance their investments.

- Commercial Loans: Commercial loans are used for purchasing commercial properties such as office buildings, retail spaces, or multifamily units. These loans have different terms and requirements compared to residential loans. Commercial loans are often based on the property's income potential and require a larger down payment.

Budgeting for Investment

Creating a comprehensive budget is essential for managing your real estate investments effectively. A well-planned budget helps you understand the financial requirements of your investment and ensures that you have sufficient funds to cover all expenses. Here are key components to include in your budget:

- Initial Costs: Estimate the initial costs of acquiring a property, including the down payment, closing costs, inspection fees, appraisal fees, and any other upfront expenses. These costs can vary depending on the property type, location, and financing terms.

- Renovation and Repair Costs: If you plan to renovate or repair the property, include these costs in your budget. Obtain quotes from contractors and factor in contingencies for unexpected expenses. Consider the scope of work, materials, labor, and permits required for the renovations.

- Ongoing Expenses: Account for ongoing expenses associated with owning and managing the property. These expenses include property taxes, insurance, property management fees, maintenance and repairs, utilities, and homeowner association (HOA) fees if applicable. Estimate these costs based on historical data and market trends.

- Reserves: Set aside reserves for potential

vacancies and unexpected repairs. Having a financial cushion ensures that you can cover expenses during periods of low occupancy or unforeseen maintenance issues. Aim to have reserves equivalent to three to six months of operating expenses.

- Financing Costs: Include the costs of financing your investment, such as mortgage payments, interest, and loan fees. Understand the terms of your financing agreement and calculate the monthly payments to ensure they fit within your budget.

Creating a detailed budget provides a clear picture of the financial requirements and potential returns of your investment. It helps you make informed decisions, manage cash flow effectively, and avoid financial strain.

Understanding Cash Flow

Cash flow is a critical aspect of real estate investing. Positive cash flow occurs when the rental income generated from a property exceeds the expenses, resulting in a profit. Negative cash flow, on the other hand, occurs when expenses exceed rental income, leading to a loss. Understanding and managing cash flow is essential for long-term success. Here's how to analyze and optimize cash flow:

- Calculate Gross Rental Income: Start by calculating the gross rental income, which is the total rent collected from tenants. Consider factors such as rental rates, occupancy rates, and potential rent increases over time. Research the local rental market to ensure your rental rates are competitive and aligned with market trends.

- Estimate Operating Expenses: Estimate the operating expenses associated with managing the property. These expenses include property taxes, insurance, property management fees, maintenance and repairs, utilities, and HOA fees. Be thorough in identifying all potential expenses to avoid underestimating costs.

- Determine Net Operating Income (NOI): Net operating income is the gross rental income minus operating expenses. NOI provides a clear picture of the property's profitability before accounting for financing costs. A positive NOI indicates that the property generates sufficient income to cover its operating expenses.

- Account for Financing Costs: Deduct the financing costs, including mortgage payments, interest, and loan fees, from the NOI to determine the net cash flow. This calculation provides a realistic view of the property's cash flow after accounting for all expenses. Positive net cash flow indicates a profitable investment, while negative cash flow suggests a need for further analysis and adjustment.

- Optimize Cash Flow: To optimize cash flow, focus on increasing rental income and reducing expenses. Consider strategies such as improving property management, implementing energy-efficient upgrades, and minimizing vacancies through effective tenant retention. Regularly review and adjust rental rates to ensure they remain competitive and aligned with market conditions.

Positive cash flow provides a stable income stream and helps build long-term wealth. It allows you to cover expenses, reinvest in your portfolio, and achieve financial independence through real estate investing. Credit and Financing Strategies

Having good credit is essential for securing favorable financing terms and maximizing your borrowing power. Lenders consider credit scores, income, and debt-to-income ratios when evaluating loan applications. Here are strategies to maintain good credit and optimize financing:

- Maintain Good Credit: Pay bills on time, reduce outstanding debt, and avoid excessive credit inquiries. Regularly monitor your credit report to identify and address any errors or discrepancies. A good credit score improves your chances of securing loans with favorable terms and lower interest rates.

- Leverage Existing Equity: If you already own properties, consider leveraging their equity to finance new acquisitions. Home equity loans, lines of credit, or cash-out refinancing can provide funds for down payments or renovations. However, be cautious and ensure that leveraging equity aligns with your overall investment strategy.

- Establish Relationships with Lenders: Build relationships with multiple lenders to access a variety of financing options. Different lenders have different criteria and loan products, so having multiple options increases your chances of finding favorable terms. Develop a strong rapport with lenders by demonstrating your financial stability and investment track record.

- Explore Creative Financing: Creative financing strategies can help you acquire properties with limited personal capital. Consider options such as seller financing, lease options, and partnerships. Seller financing involves the seller providing financing for the purchase, allowing you to bypass traditional lenders. Lease options provide the option to purchase a property after leasing it for a specified period. Partnerships allow you to pool resources and share the financial burden with other investors.

- Understand Loan Terms: Thoroughly understand the terms and conditions of any financing agreement. Pay attention to interest rates, repayment terms, prepayment penalties, and other fees. Calculate the total cost of the loan over its term and ensure that it aligns with your budget and investment goals.

Effective credit management and financing strategies are essential for building a successful real estate portfolio. By maintaining good credit, leveraging existing equity, establishing relationships with lenders, exploring creative financing options, and understanding loan terms, you can optimize your borrowing power and achieve your investment objectives.

Tax Planning and Strategies

Understanding the tax implications of real estate investing is crucial for maximizing your returns and minimizing your tax liability. Real estate investments offer various tax benefits, such as deductions for mortgage interest, property taxes, insurance, repairs, and depreciation. Here are key tax planning strategies for real estate investors:

- Deductible Expenses: Identify and deduct eligible expenses associated with your real estate investments. These expenses include mortgage interest, property taxes, insurance premiums, maintenance and repairs, property management fees, and utilities. Keep detailed records of all expenses and consult with a tax professional to ensure you maximize your deductions.

- Depreciation: Depreciation allows you to deduct a portion of the property's value each year as a tax expense. The IRS allows residential properties to be depreciated over 27.5 years and commercial properties over 39 years. Depreciation reduces your taxable income and can significantly lower your tax liability. Consult with a tax professional to calculate and claim depreciation accurately.

- 1031 Exchange: A 1031 exchange allows you to defer capital gains taxes by reinvesting the proceeds from the sale of a property into a similar property. This strategy can help you defer taxes and grow your real estate portfolio more efficiently. To qualify for a 1031 exchange, follow the IRS guidelines and work with a qualified intermediary.

- Self-Directed IRA: Consider using a self-directed IRA to invest in real estate. A self-directed IRA allows you to invest in a broader range of assets, including real estate, while enjoying the tax advantages of an IRA. Consult with a financial advisor to understand the rules and benefits of self-directed IRAs.

- Passive Activity Losses: Real estate investments are considered passive activities, and passive activity losses can offset passive income. If your real estate investments generate losses, you can use those losses to offset rental income or other passive income. This strategy can help reduce your overall tax liability.

- Capital Gains Tax: Understand the implications of capital gains tax when selling a property. Long-term capital gains (for properties held over a year) are typically taxed at lower rates than short-term gains. Consider the timing of your property sales to take advantage of favorable tax rates.

- Consult with a Tax Professional: Tax laws and

regulations are complex and subject to change. Consult with a qualified tax professional who specializes in real estate to develop a tax strategy that aligns with your investment goals. A tax professional can help you identify deductions, claim depreciation, and navigate the intricacies of real estate tax planning.

Effective tax planning can significantly enhance the profitability of your real estate investments. By identifying deductible expenses, utilizing depreciation, exploring 1031 exchanges, considering self-directed IRAs, leveraging passive activity losses, and understanding capital gains tax implications, you can optimize your after-tax returns and build wealth more efficiently.

Building a solid financial foundation is essential for successful real estate investing. By understanding real estate financing, creating a comprehensive budget, analyzing cash flow, maintaining good credit, exploring financing strategies, and implementing effective tax planning, you can build a strong financial base for your investments. Remember, financial management is an ongoing process, so continuously monitor your finances, adapt to market conditions, and seek professional advice when needed. With a solid financial foundation, you can navigate the complexities of real estate investing and achieve your financial goals.

Risk Management: Mitigating Risks in Real Estate Investment

Mitigating risks is a crucial aspect of successful real

estate investing. While real estate offers significant opportunities for wealth creation, it also involves inherent risks. Understanding and managing these risks is essential for protecting your investments and ensuring long-term success. This section explores the key elements of risk management in real estate investment and provides practical strategies for mitigating risks effectively.

Identifying and Assessing Risks

The first step in risk management is identifying and assessing the potential risks associated with real estate investment. Common risks include market fluctuations, economic downturns, property damage, tenant issues, and legal liabilities. Conduct a thorough risk assessment for each property and investment opportunity. Consider factors such as location, market conditions, property condition, tenant demographics, and potential regulatory changes. By identifying and assessing risks upfront, you can develop strategies to mitigate them effectively.

Market Risks

Market risks are related to fluctuations in property values and rental demand due to changes in the broader economic environment. These can be driven by factors such as interest rate changes, economic recessions, and shifts in supply and demand.

- Interest Rate Fluctuations: Changes in interest rates can impact your mortgage payments and the overall cost of borrowing. When interest rates rise, the cost of financing increases, which can reduce your cash flow and profitability. Conversely, lower interest rates can make borrowing cheaper and boost your returns.

- Economic Recessions: Economic downturns can lead to reduced demand for rental properties and declining property values. During recessions, tenants may face financial difficulties, leading to higher vacancy rates and lower rental income.

- Supply and Demand Shifts: Changes in the local real estate market, such as an oversupply of rental properties, can lead to increased competition and downward pressure on rental rates. Conversely, strong demand and limited supply can drive up rental rates and property values.

Property Risks

Property risks pertain to physical issues with the property itself that can impact its value, rental income, and overall profitability.

- Property Damage: Properties are susceptible to damage from natural disasters, accidents, or wear and tear. Common issues include fire, water damage, mold, and structural problems. Property damage can lead to costly repairs and potential loss of rental income.

- Maintenance and Repairs: Regular maintenance and unexpected repairs are part of property ownership. Neglecting maintenance can lead to larger issues over time, affecting tenant satisfaction and property value. Investors should budget for ongoing maintenance and set aside reserves for unexpected repairs.

Tenant Risks

Tenant risks are associated with the behavior and financial stability of tenants. These risks can impact cash flow, property condition, and legal liabilities.

- Tenant Default: Tenants may default on their rent payments due to financial difficulties or other reasons. Tenant default can lead to lost rental income, legal costs, and the time-consuming process of eviction.

- Tenant Damage: Tenants may cause damage to the property beyond normal wear and tear. This can result in costly repairs and delays in finding new tenants.

- Vacancy Risks: High vacancy rates can significantly impact cash flow and profitability. Factors contributing to vacancies include poor property condition, inadequate marketing, and high tenant turnover.

Legal and Regulatory Risks

Legal and regulatory risks arise from changes in laws and regulations that affect real estate investment. Staying compliant with local, state, and federal laws is essential for avoiding legal issues and fines.

- Zoning and Land Use Regulations: Changes in zoning laws and land use regulations can impact property use and value. Investors should stay informed about local regulations and potential changes that could affect their investments.

- Tenant-Landlord Laws: Tenant-landlord laws govern the rights and responsibilities of both parties. Violating these laws can result in legal disputes, fines, and damage to your reputation as a landlord.

- Property Taxes: Property tax assessments can change over time, affecting your operating expenses. Be aware of property tax rates in your area and factor them into your investment analysis.

Strategies for Mitigating Risks

Mitigating risks requires a proactive approach and a combination of strategies. Here are some effective risk management strategies for real estate investors: Diversification

Diversification is a fundamental risk management strategy in real estate investing. By diversifying your portfolio across different property types, locations, and markets, you can reduce the impact of market fluctuations and minimize risk. Invest in a mix of residential, commercial, and multifamily properties. Consider different geographic regions to mitigate regional risks. Diversification helps spread risk and ensures that your investment portfolio remains resilient in various market conditions. Additionally, consider investing in real estate-related assets, such as real estate investment trusts (REITs), to further diversify your holdings.

Insurance and Legal Protection

Insurance is a critical component of risk management in real estate investing. Ensure that you have adequate insurance coverage for your properties, including property insurance, liability insurance, and landlord insurance. Property insurance protects against physical damage, while liability insurance covers legal liabilities. Landlord insurance provides coverage for rental income loss, tenant-related damages, and legal expenses. Consult with an insurance professional to assess your coverage needs and obtain appropriate policies. Additionally, ensure that your lease agreements and contracts are legally sound and provide adequate protection against potential disputes and liabilities.

Tenant Screening and Management

Tenant-related risks are among the most significant challenges in real estate investing. Conduct thorough tenant screening to minimize the risk of problematic tenants. Verify tenant references, conduct background and credit checks, and ensure that tenants have a stable income. Implement a comprehensive lease agreement that outlines tenant responsibilities, rent payment terms, and maintenance expectations. Regularly inspect properties and address maintenance issues promptly to prevent property damage and ensure tenant satisfaction. Effective tenant management reduces vacancy rates, minimizes tenant turnover, and enhances the overall profitability of your investments.

Market Analysis and Adaptation

Market fluctuations and economic downturns can significantly impact real estate investments. Conduct regular market analysis to stay informed about market trends, economic indicators, and potential risks. Monitor factors such as employment rates, population growth, housing demand, and interest rates. Adapt your investment strategy based on market conditions. During economic downturns, consider focusing on properties with stable rental demand or exploring opportunities for distressed property acquisitions. By staying proactive and adapting to market changes, you can mitigate the impact of market fluctuations and position your investments for long-term success.

Maintenance and Upkeep

Regular maintenance and upkeep are essential for preserving the value of your properties and ensuring tenant satisfaction. Develop a maintenance schedule and conduct routine inspections to identify and address issues before they become major problems. Promptly address repair requests from tenants to maintain a positive landlord-tenant relationship. Keeping your properties in good condition reduces the risk of costly repairs, tenant turnover, and legal disputes.

Financial Planning and Reserves

Effective financial planning and maintaining adequate reserves are crucial for managing risks. Develop a comprehensive budget that includes all potential expenses, including property taxes, insurance, maintenance, and vacancies. Set aside reserves equivalent to three to six months of operating expenses to cover unexpected costs and periods of low occupancy. Having financial reserves provides a cushion to navigate challenges and ensures that you can meet your financial obligations.

Risk Management Tools and Resources

Leveraging tools and resources can enhance your risk management efforts. Here are some valuable tools and resources for real estate investors:
Property Management Software

Property management software streamlines property management tasks, including tenant screening, rent collection, maintenance tracking, and financial reporting. Popular property management software options include AppFolio, Buildium, and Rentec Direct. These tools help you manage your properties efficiently and reduce the risk of errors and oversights.

Real Estate Market Data and Analysis Tools

Real estate market data and analysis tools provide valuable insights into market trends, property values, and rental rates. Websites like Zillow, Realtor.com, and Redfin offer data on property values, rental rates, and market trends. Tools like CoStar and REIS provide in-depth market analysis and forecasting. Utilizing these tools helps you make informed investment decisions and stay ahead of market changes.

Legal and Tax Advisors

Consulting with legal and tax advisors is essential for navigating the complexities of real estate investing. Legal advisors can help you draft and review lease agreements, handle tenant disputes, and ensure compliance with local regulations. Tax advisors can assist with tax planning, deductions, and structuring your investments for tax efficiency. Working with qualified professionals helps you mitigate legal and tax risks.

Networking and Education

Networking with other real estate investors and professionals provides valuable insights and opportunities for collaboration. Join local real estate investment groups, attend industry conferences, and participate in online forums. Networking allows you to learn from others' experiences, share best practices, and stay informed about market trends. Additionally, invest in your education by reading books, taking online courses, and attending workshops on real estate investing.

Effective risk management is essential for long-term success in real estate investing. By identifying and assessing risks, diversifying your portfolio, obtaining adequate insurance coverage, conducting thorough tenant screening, staying informed about market trends, maintaining properties, and leveraging tools and resources, you can mitigate risks and protect your investments. Remember, risk management is an ongoing process, so continuously monitor your investments, adapt to changing circumstances, and seek professional advice when needed.

The Big Picture: Long-term Strategy for Real Estate Success

Developing a long-term strategy is essential for achieving sustained success in real estate investing. A well-defined strategy provides a roadmap for growth, profitability, and wealth accumulation. This section explores the key components of a long-term real estate strategy, offering insights and practical tips to help you build a successful and resilient investment portfolio.

Defining Your Investment Objectives

The first step in developing a long-term strategy is defining your investment objectives. Consider your financial goals, risk tolerance, and desired lifestyle. Are you seeking passive income, capital appreciation, or a combination of both? Determine the time horizon for your investments and the level of involvement you desire. Your investment objectives will guide your decision-making process and shape your overall strategy. Ensure that your objectives are specific, measurable, achievable, relevant, and time-bound (SMART).

- Passive Income: If your primary goal is to generate passive income, focus on acquiring rental properties that provide consistent cash flow. Look for properties in areas with strong rental demand and stable rental rates. Consider multifamily properties or commercial properties with long-term leases to ensure a steady income stream.

- Capital Appreciation: If you aim to achieve capital appreciation, focus on properties in high-growth areas with potential for significant value appreciation. Invest in properties that are undervalued or located in emerging markets. Consider value-add opportunities, such as properties that require renovation or repositioning, to increase their market value.

- Balanced Approach: A balanced approach combines both passive income and capital appreciation. Diversify your portfolio with a mix of rental properties that provide cash flow and properties with potential for value appreciation. This approach allows you to benefit from both steady income and long-term wealth accumulation.

Creating a Diversified Portfolio

Diversification is a cornerstone of a successful long-term strategy. Build a diversified portfolio by investing in different property types, locations, and markets. Residential properties, commercial properties, multifamily units, and real estate investment trusts (REITs) can all play a role in your portfolio. Diversification helps spread risk and reduces the impact of market fluctuations. Additionally, consider geographic diversification to mitigate regional risks. A well-diversified portfolio enhances stability and provides multiple income streams, contributing to long-term success.

- Property Types: Invest in a mix of property types, including residential, commercial, and multifamily properties. Each property type has its advantages and considerations. Residential properties provide stable rental income, while commercial properties offer longer lease terms and potential for higher returns. Multifamily properties provide multiple income streams and economies of scale.

- Geographic Locations: Diversify your investments across different geographic locations to mitigate regional risks. Consider investing in properties in different cities, states, or even countries. Geographic diversification reduces the impact of local economic downturns and market fluctuations.

- Market Segments: Explore different market segments within the real estate industry. Consider investing in niche markets such as student housing, senior living, or vacation rentals. Niche markets can offer unique opportunities and potential for higher returns.

Leveraging Technology and Data

Technology and data play a crucial role in modern real

estate investing. Leverage advanced tools and platforms to streamline your investment process, conduct market analysis, and make data-driven decisions. Utilize real estate software for property management, financial analysis, and tenant screening. Access online resources, market reports, and industry databases to gather valuable insights. By leveraging technology and data, you can enhance your efficiency, accuracy, and overall investment performance.

- Property Management Software: Property management software automates and streamlines property management tasks, including rent collection, maintenance tracking, and tenant communication. Popular property management software options include AppFolio, Buildium, and Rentec Direct. These tools help you manage your properties efficiently and reduce administrative burden.

- Market Analysis Tools: Utilize market analysis tools to gather data on property values, rental rates, and market trends. Websites like Zillow, Realtor.com, and Redfin provide valuable insights into local real estate markets. Tools like CoStar and REIS offer in-depth market analysis and forecasting. Using these tools helps you make informed investment decisions.

- Financial Analysis Software: Financial analysis software helps you evaluate the financial performance of your investments. Tools like RealPage and Stessa provide detailed financial reports, cash flow analysis, and investment tracking. Financial analysis software enables you to assess the profitability and risk of your investments accurately.

- Data Analytics: Leverage data analytics to identify trends, predict market movements, and optimize your investment strategy. Analyze data on demographic trends, economic indicators, and housing demand to identify emerging opportunities. Data-driven insights help you make informed decisions and stay ahead of market changes.

Continuous Learning and Improvement

Real estate markets are dynamic and ever-evolving, requiring continuous learning and improvement. Stay updated with the latest industry trends, regulations, and best practices. Attend real estate seminars, workshops, and conferences. Join industry associations and networking groups to connect with experienced investors and professionals. Invest in your education by reading books, taking online courses, and seeking mentorship. Continuous learning enhances your knowledge, skills, and adaptability, positioning you for long-term success in the real estate market.

- Industry Seminars and Workshops: Attend industry seminars and workshops to gain insights from experts and stay informed about the latest trends. Topics may include market analysis, investment strategies, property management, and legal issues. Seminars and workshops provide valuable networking opportunities and access to industry resources.

- Online Courses and Webinars: Online courses and webinars offer flexible learning options for real estate investors. Platforms like Udemy, Coursera, and LinkedIn Learning provide courses on various real estate topics. Online courses allow you to learn at your own pace and enhance your knowledge and skills.

- Industry Associations: Join industry associations such as the National Association of Realtors (NAR), Urban Land Institute (ULI), and Real Estate Investment Network (REIN). Membership in these associations provides access to industry publications, research reports, and networking events. Associations often offer educational programs and certifications.

- Mentorship and Networking: Seek mentorship from experienced real estate investors and professionals. A mentor can provide guidance, share insights, and help you navigate challenges. Networking with other investors allows you to learn from their experiences, share best practices, and collaborate on investment opportunities.

Exit Strategies and Legacy Planning

Having a clear exit strategy is essential for long-term success. Define your exit plan, whether it's selling properties for a profit, refinancing to access equity, or passing on your portfolio to future generations. Consider the timing and market conditions for executing your exit strategy. Additionally, plan for your real estate legacy by establishing a comprehensive estate plan. Ensure that your properties are properly titled, and consider setting up trusts or other legal structures to facilitate a smooth transfer of assets. By having a well-defined exit strategy and legacy plan, you can maximize your returns and ensure the long-term sustainability of your investments.

- Selling Properties: Selling properties for a profit is a common exit strategy. Consider market conditions, property appreciation, and tax implications when planning to sell. Timing the sale to capitalize on market peaks can maximize your returns. Work with real estate agents and brokers to market your properties effectively.

- Refinancing: Refinancing allows you to access the equity in your properties without selling them. By refinancing, you can obtain cash for new investments, renovations, or other financial needs. Assess current interest rates and loan terms to determine if refinancing is a viable option. Consult with lenders to explore refinancing options.

- Legacy Planning: Plan for the long-term sustainability of your real estate portfolio by establishing an estate plan. Consider setting up trusts, family limited partnerships, or other legal structures to facilitate the transfer of assets to future generations. Work with estate planning attorneys and financial advisors to develop a comprehensive legacy plan. Ensure that your properties are properly titled and that your estate plan reflects your wishes.

- Tax Efficiency: Consider the tax implications of your exit strategy. Long-term capital gains are typically taxed at lower rates than short-term gains. Explore tax-efficient strategies such as 1031 exchanges, which allow you to defer capital gains taxes by reinvesting the proceeds from the sale of a property into a similar property. Consult with tax advisors to optimize your tax strategy.

Monitoring and Adapting Your Strategy

Long-term success in real estate investing requires ongoing monitoring and adaptation. Regularly review the performance of your portfolio, assess market conditions, and adjust your strategy as needed. Stay informed about economic trends, regulatory changes, and market developments. Continuously refine your investment approach to align with your evolving goals and market opportunities.

- Portfolio Performance: Monitor the performance of your real estate portfolio regularly. Analyze key metrics such as cash flow, occupancy rates, rental income, and property appreciation. Identify underperforming properties and develop strategies to improve their performance. Regularly review your financial statements and reports.

- Market Conditions: Stay informed about local and national market conditions. Monitor economic indicators, housing demand, interest rates, and market trends. Adjust your investment strategy based on market conditions to capitalize on emerging opportunities and mitigate risks.

- Regulatory Changes: Keep abreast of regulatory changes that may impact your real estate investments. Changes in zoning laws, tenant-landlord regulations, tax policies, and environmental regulations can affect your properties. Stay informed about regulatory developments and adapt your strategy accordingly.

- Strategic Adjustments: Be willing to make strategic adjustments to your investment approach. If market conditions change or new opportunities arise, reassess your goals and objectives. Flexibility and adaptability are key to long-term success in real estate investing.

Developing a long-term strategy is essential for achieving sustained success in real estate investing. By defining your investment objectives, creating a diversified portfolio, leveraging technology and data, continuously learning and improving, planning for exit and legacy, and monitoring and adapting your strategy, you can build a successful and resilient real estate investment portfolio. Remember, real estate investing is a long-term journey, so stay focused, adapt to changing conditions, and remain committed to your goals.

Chapter 2:

Getting Started in Real Estate Investing

Embarking on a journey in real estate investing is an exciting and rewarding endeavor. For many, real estate represents a pathway to financial independence, wealth accumulation, and the ability to create a passive income stream. This section will explore the advantages of investing in rental properties, providing insights into why real estate is an attractive investment choice.

Why Real Estate?: Advantages of Investing in Rental Properties

Investing in rental properties offers numerous benefits that make it an appealing option for investors. These advantages include the potential for steady cash flow, long-term appreciation, tax benefits, diversification, and the ability to leverage financing. Let's delve into each of these advantages to understand why real estate is a compelling investment.

Steady Cash Flow

One of the primary reasons investors are drawn to rental properties is the potential for steady cash flow. Rental properties generate regular income through monthly rent payments from tenants. This income stream can provide financial stability and help cover the property's operating expenses, mortgage payments, and maintenance costs. The surplus income, known as positive cash flow, can be used for reinvestment, savings, or personal expenses.

- Consistent Income Stream: Unlike other investments that may not generate regular income, rental properties offer a consistent income stream. As long as the property is occupied, rental income is typically reliable and predictable. This steady cash flow can help investors achieve financial independence and build wealth over time.

- Inflation Hedge: Rental income tends to increase over time, often in line with inflation. As the cost of living rises, so do rental rates, allowing investors to maintain their purchasing power. This inflation-hedged income stream provides a level of financial security that other investments may not offer.

- Income Stability: During economic downturns, rental properties can offer income stability. While other investments may experience volatility and declining returns, rental properties can continue to generate income, especially in markets with high demand for rental housing.

Long-term Appreciation

In addition to generating steady cash flow, rental properties have the potential for long-term appreciation. Property values tend to increase over time, driven by factors such as population growth, economic development, and inflation. This appreciation can significantly enhance an investor's wealth and provide substantial returns on investment.

- Capital Gains: When property values appreciate, investors can realize capital gains by selling the property at a higher price than the purchase price. These gains can be substantial, especially in high-growth markets. Real estate appreciation can be a powerful wealth-building tool, enabling investors to achieve significant returns on their initial investment.

- Equity Buildup: As property values increase, so does the equity in the property. Equity is the difference between the property's market value and the outstanding mortgage balance. Over time, as investors pay down their mortgage and property values appreciate, their equity in the property grows. This equity can be leveraged to finance additional investments or used as collateral for other financial needs.

- Forced Appreciation: Investors can also achieve forced appreciation by improving the property's condition and value. Renovations, upgrades, and effective property management can increase the property's market value, leading to higher rental income and potential resale value. Forced appreciation allows investors to actively enhance their returns through strategic property improvements.

Tax Benefits

Real estate investing offers various tax benefits that can enhance an investor's overall returns. These tax advantages include deductions for mortgage interest, property taxes, depreciation, and other expenses related to property management and maintenance.

- Mortgage Interest Deduction: Investors can deduct the interest paid on their mortgage loans, reducing their taxable income. This deduction can be significant, especially in the early years of the mortgage when interest payments are higher.

- Depreciation: Depreciation is a non-cash expense that allows investors to deduct a portion of the property's value each year for tax purposes. The IRS allows residential properties to be depreciated over 27.5 years and commercial properties over 39 years. Depreciation reduces taxable income, resulting in lower tax liability and higher after-tax returns.

- Operating Expense Deductions: Investors can deduct various operating expenses, such as property management fees, maintenance and repairs, insurance premiums, utilities, and marketing costs. These deductions help offset rental income and reduce overall tax liability.

1031 Exchange: A 1031 exchange allows investors to defer capital gains taxes by reinvesting the proceeds from the sale of a property into a similar property. This strategy can help investors defer taxes and grow their real estate portfolio more efficiently. By utilizing a 1031 exchange, investors can preserve their capital and reinvest it in higher-value properties.

Diversification

Real estate investing provides an excellent opportunity for portfolio diversification. Diversifying investments across different asset classes can help reduce risk and enhance overall returns. Rental properties offer diversification benefits that can complement traditional investments such as stocks, bonds, and mutual funds.

- Low Correlation with Other Assets: Real estate has a low correlation with other asset classes, meaning its performance is not directly tied to the stock market or bond market. This low correlation helps reduce overall portfolio volatility and risk. During periods of market turbulence, real estate can provide stability and consistent returns.

- Income Diversification: Adding rental properties to an investment portfolio diversifies income sources. Rental income provides a steady cash flow that is not dependent on the performance of other investments. This income diversification can enhance financial security and reduce reliance on any single income stream.

- Asset Stability: Real estate is a tangible asset

that tends to hold its value over time. Unlike stocks and bonds, which can fluctuate significantly in value, real estate offers stability and intrinsic value. This stability makes real estate a reliable long-term investment that can withstand economic cycles and market fluctuations.

Leverage Financing

One of the unique advantages of real estate investing is the ability to leverage financing. Leverage allows investors to use borrowed capital to acquire properties, magnifying their potential returns. By using other people's money (OPM), investors can control more assets and increase their investment power.

- Higher Returns on Equity: Leverage can enhance returns on equity (ROE) by allowing investors to earn returns on the total value of the property, not just their initial investment. For example, if an investor puts down 20% of the property's purchase price and finances the remaining 80% with a mortgage, they can earn returns on the entire property's value. This leverage can significantly boost overall returns and accelerate wealth accumulation.

- Real Estate as Collateral: Real estate serves as collateral for financing, making it easier to obtain loans with favorable terms. Lenders view real estate as a relatively low-risk asset, allowing investors to secure financing at competitive interest rates. This access to financing provides flexibility and opportunities for expanding the real estate portfolio.

- Cash Flow Amplification: Leveraging financing can amplify cash flow by allowing investors to acquire multiple properties. Instead of using all available capital to purchase one property, investors can spread their capital across several properties, increasing rental income and overall cash flow. This strategy enables investors to scale their investments and build a diversified portfolio.

Inflation Protection

Real estate investing offers a natural hedge against inflation. As the cost of living rises, so do property values and rental rates. This inflation protection helps preserve the purchasing power of an investor's income and assets.

- Rental Income Growth: Rental rates tend to increase with inflation, ensuring that rental income keeps pace with rising costs. This income growth provides a stable and inflation-hedged cash flow that can support long-term financial goals.

- Property Value Appreciation: Property values generally increase with inflation, protecting the value of the investment. Real estate's intrinsic value as a physical asset helps preserve its worth over time, making it a reliable store of wealth.

- Debt Repayment with Inflation: Inflation erodes the real value of debt, making it easier to repay loans with devalued dollars. As inflation increases, the real burden of mortgage payments decreases, benefiting leveraged investors. This dynamic allows investors to effectively repay debt with future income that has higher nominal value.

Control and Flexibility

Investing in rental properties offers a high degree of control and flexibility compared to other investment options. Real estate investors have the ability to make strategic decisions that directly impact the performance and profitability of their investments.

- Property Management: Investors can choose to manage properties themselves or hire professional property managers. This control over property management allows investors to maintain the property, set rental rates, and select tenants. Effective property management can enhance tenant satisfaction, reduce vacancies, and maximize rental income.

- Value-Add Opportunities: Real estate investors can actively increase the value of their properties through renovations, upgrades, and strategic improvements. These value-add opportunities provide flexibility to enhance returns and achieve higher property appreciation. Investors can also reposition properties to meet changing market demands and attract higher-paying tenants.

- Portfolio Customization: Real estate investors have the flexibility to customize their investment portfolios to align with their financial goals and risk tolerance. Whether focusing on residential, commercial, or multifamily properties, investors can tailor their portfolios to suit their preferences and investment strategies. This customization allows for a personalized approach to real estate investing.

- Exit Strategies: Real estate offers multiple exit strategies, providing flexibility in managing investments. Investors can choose to sell properties for a profit, refinance to access equity, or hold properties for long-term income. These exit strategies allow investors to adapt to changing market conditions and personal financial goals.
- Wealth Building and Legacy Creation

Real estate investing is a powerful tool for building wealth and creating a lasting legacy. The combination of steady cash flow, property appreciation, tax benefits, and leverage can significantly enhance an investor's net worth and financial security.

- Equity Growth: Over time, as properties appreciate and mortgage balances decrease, investors build substantial equity. This equity represents the ownership value in the property and can be leveraged for future investments or financial needs. Building equity through real estate is a reliable pathway to wealth accumulation.

- Generational Wealth: Real estate investments can be passed down to future generations, creating a lasting legacy. Properties can provide long-term income and financial security for heirs. Establishing a comprehensive estate plan ensures that real estate assets are transferred smoothly and efficiently to future generations.

- Passive Income: Rental properties generate passive income, allowing investors to achieve financial independence and enjoy a comfortable lifestyle. This passive income stream can support personal goals, retirement plans, and philanthropic endeavors. Real estate investing provides the means to achieve financial freedom and pursue one's passions.

Community Impact

Real estate investing offers the opportunity to make a positive impact on communities. By providing quality housing and improving properties, investors contribute to the overall well-being and development of neighborhoods.

- Housing Availability: Real estate investors play a vital role in providing housing options for individuals and families. By investing in rental properties, investors help meet the demand for affordable and quality housing. This contribution is especially important in areas with housing shortages or high rental demand.

- Neighborhood Revitalization: Real estate investors can contribute to the revitalization of neighborhoods by improving properties and enhancing their appeal. Renovating and maintaining properties can uplift the surrounding area, attract new residents, and stimulate economic growth. This positive impact benefits both the community and the investor.

- Sustainable Practices: Investors can implement sustainable practices in property management, such as energy-efficient upgrades, water conservation measures, and eco-friendly building materials. These practices reduce the environmental footprint of properties and promote sustainability. By adopting green initiatives, investors contribute to a healthier and more sustainable future.

Investing in rental properties offers numerous advantages that make it an attractive option for investors. The potential for steady cash flow, long-term appreciation, tax benefits, diversification, leverage, inflation protection, control, and wealth building are compelling reasons to consider real estate as a cornerstone of your investment portfolio. By understanding and leveraging these advantages, investors can achieve financial independence, build wealth, and create a lasting legacy. Real estate investing is a journey that offers both financial rewards and the opportunity to make a positive impact on communities. With careful planning, strategic decision-making, and a commitment to continuous learning, you can embark on a successful real estate investment journey and achieve your financial goals.

Types of Properties: Residential vs. Commercial

When it comes to real estate investing, one of the key decisions you'll make is choosing between residential and commercial properties. Each type of property comes with its own set of advantages, challenges, and market dynamics. Understanding the differences between these two categories is crucial for aligning your investment strategy with your financial goals. This section will explore the characteristics, benefits, and considerations for both residential and commercial properties, helping you make an informed decision on which type of property to invest in.

Residential Properties

Residential properties are buildings or units designed for people to live in. They include single-family homes, multi-family properties, condominiums, townhouses, and apartments. Residential real estate is often seen as a more straightforward entry point for new investors due to its familiarity and the steady demand for housing.

Types of Residential Properties

- Single-Family Homes: These are standalone properties designed to house one family. Single-family homes are popular among first-time investors because they are relatively easy to manage and finance. They offer good liquidity, as there is typically a large pool of potential buyers and renters.

- Multi-Family Properties: These include duplexes, triplexes, and apartment buildings with multiple units. Multi-family properties provide higher rental income due to the multiple streams of rent. They also offer economies of scale, making them more cost-effective to manage on a per-unit basis.

- Condominiums: Condos are individual units within a larger building or complex, with shared common areas. They are often more affordable than single-family homes and come with lower maintenance responsibilities, as the homeowners' association (HOA) manages common areas.

- Townhouses: These are multi-story homes that share one or more walls with adjacent properties. Townhouses combine the benefits of single-family homes and condos, offering more space than condos while still being part of a community with shared amenities.

Benefits of Residential Properties

- Steady Demand: There is a consistent demand for housing, making residential properties a relatively stable investment. People always need a place to live, regardless of economic conditions, which provides a steady stream of potential tenants.

- Easier Financing: Residential properties often have more financing options available, including conventional mortgages, FHA loans, and VA loans. These loans typically come with lower interest rates and longer repayment terms, making them more accessible for investors.

- Lower Entry Barriers: Residential properties usually require a lower initial investment compared to commercial properties. This makes them more accessible for new investors with limited capital.

- Simplicity: Managing residential properties is generally simpler than commercial properties. The lease agreements are more straightforward, and the maintenance and management tasks are less complex.

- Tax Benefits: Investors in residential properties can benefit from various tax deductions, including mortgage interest, property taxes, and depreciation.
- Considerations for Residential Properties

- Tenant Turnover: Residential properties may experience higher tenant turnover rates compared to commercial properties. Frequent turnover can lead to increased vacancy periods and additional costs associated with finding new tenants.

- Rental Income: While residential properties provide steady rental income, the rental yields are generally lower compared to commercial properties. Investors may need to own multiple residential properties to achieve their desired income levels.

- Property Management: Managing multiple residential properties can be time-consuming and may require hiring a property management company. This adds to the overall cost of maintaining the investment.

- Market Sensitivity: Residential property values can be more sensitive to local market conditions and economic cycles. Factors such as employment rates, interest rates, and housing supply can significantly impact property values and rental demand.

Commercial Properties

Commercial properties are buildings or spaces used for business purposes. They include office buildings, retail spaces, industrial properties, warehouses, and mixed-use developments. Commercial real estate often offers higher returns and longer lease terms compared to residential properties, but it also comes with higher risks and more complex management requirements.

Types of Commercial Properties

Office Buildings: These are properties designed for businesses to conduct their operations. Office buildings can range from small single-tenant buildings to large multi-tenant skyscrapers. They are typically located in business districts or commercial zones.

- Retail Spaces: Retail properties include shopping centers, strip malls, standalone stores, and restaurants. They are designed to house businesses that sell goods and services directly to consumers.

- Industrial Properties: These properties are used for manufacturing, production, storage, and distribution. Industrial properties include factories, warehouses, and distribution centers.

- Warehouses: Warehouses are large storage facilities used for storing goods and products. They are often located near transportation hubs for easy distribution.

- Mixed-Use Developments: These properties combine multiple uses, such as residential, commercial, and retail, within a single development. Mixed-use properties offer diversified income streams and can enhance the overall value of the investment.
- Benefits of Commercial Properties

- Higher Rental Income: Commercial properties typically offer higher rental yields compared to residential properties. Businesses are often willing to pay premium rents for prime locations and quality spaces.

- Longer Lease Terms: Commercial leases tend to be longer than residential leases, often ranging from five to ten years or more. Longer lease terms provide stable and predictable income for investors.

- Triple Net Leases: Many commercial properties use triple net (NNN) leases, where the tenant is responsible for paying property taxes, insurance, and maintenance costs. This reduces the landlord's operating expenses and increases the net income.

- Diversification: Investing in commercial properties can diversify an investment portfolio, reducing reliance on residential markets and providing exposure to different economic sectors.

- Appreciation Potential: Commercial properties in prime locations can experience significant appreciation over time, driven by factors such as economic growth, infrastructure development, and increasing demand for business spaces.
- Considerations for Commercial Properties

- Higher Entry Barriers: Commercial properties typically require a larger initial investment compared to residential properties. The higher cost can be a barrier for new investors with limited capital.

- Complex Financing: Financing commercial properties can be more complex and may involve higher interest rates and shorter loan terms. Lenders often require a larger down payment and more stringent qualification criteria.

- Market Volatility: Commercial real estate markets can be more volatile and sensitive to economic cycles. Factors such as changes in consumer behavior, technological advancements, and economic downturns can impact the demand for commercial spaces.

- Management Complexity: Managing commercial properties can be more complex due to the specialized nature of the spaces and the needs of business tenants. Property management may require more expertise and resources.

- Tenant Risks: The financial stability of business tenants can impact the income from commercial properties. Economic downturns or changes in the business environment can lead to tenant bankruptcies and vacancies.

Choosing between residential and commercial properties depends on your investment goals, risk tolerance, and available capital. Both types of properties offer unique advantages and challenges, and a well-rounded real estate portfolio may include a mix of both. By understanding the characteristics and market dynamics of residential and commercial properties, you can make informed investment decisions and build a successful real estate portfolio. Understanding Market Trends: Research and Analysis

Understanding market trends is a critical aspect of

successful real estate investing. Market trends provide insights into the current and future state of the real estate market, helping investors make informed decisions about when and where to invest. This section will explore the importance of market research and analysis, key market indicators to monitor, and strategies for conducting effective market analysis. Importance of Market Research and Analysis

Market research and analysis are essential for identifying investment opportunities, assessing risks, and making strategic decisions. Here are some key reasons why market research and analysis are important:

- Identifying Investment Opportunities: Market research helps investors identify emerging markets, undervalued properties, and high-growth areas. By analyzing market trends, investors can pinpoint locations with strong demand, favorable economic conditions, and potential for appreciation.

- Assessing Market Conditions: Understanding market conditions allows investors to gauge the supply and demand dynamics, rental rates, and property values. This information is crucial for determining the feasibility and profitability of an investment.

- Mitigating Risks: Market analysis helps investors identify potential risks, such as market saturation, economic downturns, and regulatory changes. By understanding these risks, investors can develop strategies to mitigate them and protect their investments.

- Strategic Planning: Comprehensive market analysis provides the foundation for strategic planning. Investors can set realistic goals, develop investment strategies, and allocate resources effectively based on market insights.

- Staying Competitive: Keeping up with market trends allows investors to stay competitive and adapt to changing market conditions. Timely and accurate market information enables investors to make proactive decisions and capitalize on emerging opportunities.

Key Market Indicators to Monitor

Monitoring key market indicators is essential for understanding the current state and future direction of the real estate market. Here are some critical market indicators to consider:

Economic Indicators

- Gross Domestic Product (GDP): GDP measures the overall economic output of a region. Strong GDP growth indicates a healthy economy, which can drive demand for real estate. Investors should monitor GDP trends to assess the economic health of their target markets.

- Employment Rates: Employment rates provide insights into the job market and economic stability. High employment rates and job growth contribute to increased demand for housing and commercial spaces. Investors should focus on areas with strong employment trends and diverse job opportunities.

- Income Levels: Median household income levels reflect the purchasing power and affordability of a region. Higher income levels support higher rental rates and property values. Investors should analyze income trends to assess the financial capacity of potential tenants.

- Interest Rates: Interest rates impact the cost of borrowing and the overall affordability of real estate. Lower interest rates can stimulate demand for properties, while higher rates can dampen demand. Investors should stay informed about interest rate trends and monetary policies.

Real Estate Market Indicators

- Median Home Prices: Median home prices indicate the overall price level of properties in a market. Rising home prices suggest strong demand and potential for appreciation, while declining prices may indicate market saturation or economic challenges.

- Rental Rates: Rental rates reflect the income potential of rental properties. Analyzing rental rate trends helps investors determine the feasibility of generating positive cash flow. High rental rates relative to property values indicate strong rental demand and profitability.

- Vacancy Rates: Vacancy rates measure the percentage of unoccupied rental properties. Low vacancy rates indicate high demand and rental stability, while high vacancy rates suggest oversupply and potential income challenges. Investors should target markets with low vacancy rates to ensure consistent rental income.

- Days on Market (DOM): DOM measures the average time it takes for properties to sell. A low DOM indicates a competitive market with high demand, while a high DOM suggests a slower market. Monitoring DOM helps investors gauge market liquidity and the ease of selling properties.

- Inventory Levels: Inventory levels represent the number of available properties for sale or rent. Low inventory levels indicate limited supply and potential for price appreciation, while high inventory levels suggest market saturation and downward pressure on prices.

- Cap Rates: Capitalization rates (cap rates) measure the potential return on investment for rental properties. A higher cap rate indicates a higher potential return but may also involve higher risk. Investors should balance cap rates with market stability and growth potential.

Demographic Indicators

Population Growth: Population growth drives demand

for housing and commercial spaces. Investors should target areas with positive population growth trends, as this indicates a growing market with increased demand for real estate.

- Age Distribution: Age distribution provides insights into the demographic profile of a region. For example, areas with a high concentration of young professionals may have strong demand for rental properties, while regions with an aging population may require more senior housing options.

- Household Composition: Household composition, such as the number of families, single individuals, and multi-generational households, influences housing demand and preferences. Understanding household trends helps investors tailor their property offerings to meet market needs.

- Migration Patterns: Migration patterns, including inbound and outbound migration, impact real estate demand. Areas experiencing net inbound migration are likely to have increased demand for housing, while areas with net outbound migration may face declining demand.

Strategies for Conducting Effective Market Analysis

Conducting effective market analysis requires a systematic approach and the use of various tools and resources. Here are some strategies for conducting thorough market research and analysis:

Primary Research

- Surveys and Questionnaires: Conduct surveys and questionnaires to gather direct feedback from potential tenants, buyers, and local residents. This primary research provides valuable insights into market preferences, demand, and satisfaction levels.

- Interviews and Focus Groups: Conduct interviews and focus groups with real estate professionals, property managers, and local business owners. These discussions provide qualitative insights into market trends, challenges, and opportunities.

- Site Visits: Visit the target market to observe the neighborhood, assess property conditions, and gather firsthand information. Site visits help investors understand the local market dynamics and make informed decisions.

Secondary Research

- Market Reports and Publications: Access market reports and publications from reputable sources such as real estate research firms, industry associations, and government agencies. These reports provide comprehensive data and analysis on market trends, property values, and economic indicators.

- Online Real Estate Platforms: Utilize online

real estate platforms such as Zillow, Realtor.com, and Redfin to gather data on property listings, prices, rental rates, and market trends. These platforms offer valuable tools for analyzing market conditions.

- Industry Databases: Access industry databases such as CoStar, REIS, and LoopNet for detailed market analysis and forecasting. These databases provide extensive data on commercial real estate markets, including vacancy rates, cap rates, and lease trends.

- Government Data: Utilize government data sources such as the U.S. Census Bureau, Bureau of Labor Statistics, and local planning departments for demographic, economic, and housing data. Government data provides reliable and up-to-date information for market analysis.

Comparative Market Analysis (CMA)

- Identify Comparable Properties: Identify properties similar to the one you are analyzing in terms of location, size, condition, and amenities. These comparable properties (comps) provide a benchmark for assessing property values and rental rates.

- Analyze Sales and Rental Data: Analyze recent sales and rental data for comparable properties to determine market value and rental income potential. Look for trends in pricing, days on market, and rental rates to gauge market conditions.

- Adjust for Differences: Adjust the data for differences between the subject property and comparable properties. Consider factors such as property condition, upgrades, and unique features that may impact value and rental income.

Trend Analysis

- Historical Data: Analyze historical data to identify long-term trends and patterns in property values, rental rates, and market conditions. Historical data provides context for understanding current market dynamics and forecasting future trends.

- Seasonal Trends: Consider seasonal trends that may impact the real estate market. For example, housing demand may increase during certain times of the year, such as spring and summer, leading to higher prices and shorter days on market.

- Economic Cycles: Understand the impact of economic cycles on the real estate market. Real estate markets are influenced by broader economic conditions, including recessions, recoveries, and periods of economic growth. Analyzing economic cycles helps investors anticipate market changes and make strategic decisions.

Geographic Information Systems (GIS)

- Mapping and Spatial Analysis: Utilize Geographic Information Systems (GIS) to map and analyze spatial data. GIS tools allow investors to visualize market trends, population density, transportation networks, and other geographic factors that influence real estate demand.

- Heat Maps: Create heat maps to identify areas with high demand, price appreciation, and rental income potential. Heat maps provide a visual representation of market hotspots and help investors target the most promising locations.

- Proximity Analysis: Conduct proximity analysis to assess the impact of nearby amenities, schools, transportation hubs, and commercial centers on property values and rental demand. Proximity to key amenities can significantly enhance the attractiveness of a property.

Professional Networks

- Real Estate Agents and Brokers: Collaborate with local real estate agents and brokers who have in-depth knowledge of the market. Agents and brokers can provide valuable insights, market data, and access to off-market deals.

- Property Managers: Engage with property managers to understand rental trends, tenant preferences, and occupancy rates. Property managers have hands-on experience with managing rental properties and can provide practical insights into market conditions.

- Industry Associations: Join industry associations such as the National Association of Realtors (NAR), Urban Land Institute (ULI), and local real estate investment groups. These associations offer resources, research reports, and networking opportunities to stay informed about market trends.

- Networking Events: Attend real estate conferences, seminars, and networking events to connect with other investors, professionals, and industry experts. Networking provides opportunities to share knowledge, gain insights, and discover investment opportunities.

Understanding market trends through comprehensive research and analysis is essential for successful real estate investing. By monitoring key market indicators, conducting primary and secondary research, performing comparative market analysis, analyzing trends, utilizing GIS tools, and leveraging professional networks, investors can make informed decisions and capitalize on emerging opportunities. Market research and analysis provide the foundation for strategic planning, risk mitigation, and long-term success in the real estate market. With a thorough understanding of market trends, investors can navigate the complexities of real estate investing and achieve their financial goals.

Building a Real Estate Team: Key Players You Need

Successful real estate investing is rarely a solo endeavor. It involves collaboration with a team of professionals who bring diverse skills and expertise to the table. Building a strong real estate team is crucial for navigating the complexities of the market, managing properties effectively, and maximizing returns. This section will explore the key players you need on your real estate team, including their roles, responsibilities, and how to choose the right professionals.

Real Estate Agent or Broker

A real estate agent or broker is often the first point of contact for investors. These professionals help you find and acquire properties that match your investment criteria.

Roles and Responsibilities:

- Property Search: Real estate agents or brokers assist in identifying properties that meet your investment goals. They have access to Multiple Listing Services (MLS) and off-market deals.

- Market Analysis: Agents provide insights into local market trends, property values, and neighborhood dynamics. They help you make informed decisions based on current market conditions.

- Negotiation: Agents negotiate on your behalf to

secure the best possible purchase price and terms. Their negotiation skills can save you money and mitigate risks.

- Transaction Management: Agents handle the paperwork and legal aspects of the transaction, ensuring compliance with local regulations and a smooth closing process.

Choosing the Right Agent or Broker:

- Experience: Look for agents with experience in real estate investing and a track record of successful transactions.

- Market Knowledge: Choose agents who specialize in the geographic area and property type you are interested in.

- Reputation: Check references, reviews, and professional affiliations to ensure the agent has a good reputation.

- Communication: Effective communication is key. Ensure the agent is responsive, proactive, and understands your investment goals.

Real Estate Attorney

A real estate attorney provides legal guidance and ensures that your transactions comply with local, state, and federal laws.

Roles and Responsibilities:

- Contract Review: Attorneys review purchase agreements, lease agreements, and other legal documents to protect your interests.

- Title Search: They conduct title searches to ensure the property has a clear title, free of liens or legal disputes.

- Closing: Attorneys oversee the closing process, ensuring all legal requirements are met and handling the transfer of ownership.

- Dispute Resolution: They assist in resolving legal disputes related to property transactions, tenant issues, or zoning regulations.

Choosing the Right Attorney:

- Specialization: Choose an attorney who specializes in real estate law and has experience with investment properties.

- Local Knowledge: Ensure the attorney is familiar with local real estate laws and regulations.

- Reputation: Check references and reviews to verify the attorney's reputation and reliability.

- Accessibility: Choose an attorney who is accessible and responsive to your needs.

Mortgage Broker or Lender

A mortgage broker or lender helps you secure financing for your real estate investments.

Roles and Responsibilities:

- Loan Options: Brokers and lenders provide access to various loan products, including conventional loans, FHA loans, VA loans, and commercial loans.

- Pre-Approval: They assist in getting pre-approved for a mortgage, which strengthens your position as a buyer.

- Rate Comparison: Brokers compare interest rates and loan terms from different lenders to find the best financing options.

- Loan Processing: They guide you through the loan application process, from submission to approval and closing.

Choosing the Right Broker or Lender:

- Experience: Look for brokers or lenders with experience in real estate investment financing.

- Loan Products: Ensure they offer a wide range of loan products that suit your investment strategy.

- Reputation: Check reviews, references, and professional affiliations to verify their credibility.

- Customer Service: Choose a broker or lender who provides excellent customer service and clear communication.

Property Manager

A property manager handles the day-to-day operations of your rental properties, ensuring they are well-maintained and profitable.

Roles and Responsibilities:

- Tenant Screening: Property managers conduct background checks, verify references, and select qualified tenants.

- Rent Collection: They manage rent collection, ensuring timely payments and handling delinquent accounts.

- Maintenance and Repairs: Property managers coordinate maintenance and repairs, addressing issues promptly to keep properties in good condition.

- Tenant Relations: They handle tenant inquiries, complaints, and lease renewals, maintaining positive tenant relationships.

- Financial Reporting: Property managers provide regular financial reports, detailing income, expenses, and property performance.

Choosing the Right Property Manager:

- Experience: Look for property managers with experience managing similar properties in your target market.

- Certifications: Choose managers with professional certifications from organizations like the Institute of Real Estate Management (IREM) or the National Association of Residential Property Managers (NARPM).

- Reputation: Check references, reviews, and client testimonials to ensure they have a good track record.

- Management Agreement: Review the management agreement carefully to understand their fees, services, and responsibilities.

Accountant or CPA

An accountant or Certified Public Accountant (CPA) helps you manage the financial aspects of your real estate investments, including tax planning and compliance.

Roles and Responsibilities:

- Bookkeeping: Accountants handle bookkeeping, ensuring accurate financial records for your properties.

- Tax Preparation: They prepare and file tax

returns, maximizing deductions and ensuring compliance with tax laws.

- Financial Analysis: Accountants provide financial analysis, helping you understand cash flow, profitability, and return on investment (ROI).

- Tax Planning: They offer tax planning strategies to minimize your tax liability and maximize your after-tax returns.

Choosing the Right Accountant or CPA:

- Specialization: Choose an accountant who specializes in real estate and has experience with investment properties.

- Certifications: Ensure they are a licensed CPA with professional affiliations.

- Reputation: Check references, reviews, and client testimonials to verify their credibility.

- Communication: Choose an accountant who communicates clearly and provides timely updates on your financial matters.

Contractor or Handyman

A reliable contractor or handyman is essential for maintaining and improving your properties.

Roles and Responsibilities:

- Repairs and Maintenance: Contractors handle routine repairs and maintenance tasks, keeping your properties in good condition.

- Renovations and Upgrades: They manage renovation projects, from minor upgrades to major remodels, to enhance property value and appeal.

- Emergency Repairs: Contractors provide emergency repair services to address urgent issues promptly.

Choosing the Right Contractor or Handyman:

- Experience: Look for contractors with experience in real estate investment properties and a portfolio of completed projects.

- Licensing and Insurance: Ensure they are licensed and insured to protect against liability and ensure quality workmanship.

- Reputation: Check references, reviews, and client testimonials to verify their reliability and quality of work.

- Cost and Availability: Choose a contractor who offers competitive pricing and is available to meet your maintenance and renovation needs.

Insurance Agent

An insurance agent helps you secure the appropriate insurance coverage for your properties, protecting your investments from risks.

Roles and Responsibilities:

- Policy Selection: Insurance agents help you choose the right insurance policies, including property insurance, liability insurance, and landlord insurance.

- Coverage Assessment: They assess your coverage needs based on the property type, location, and potential risks.

- Claims Assistance: Insurance agents assist with filing claims and navigating the claims process in case of damage or loss.

Choosing the Right Insurance Agent:

- Experience: Look for insurance agents with experience in real estate investment properties.

- Product Knowledge: Ensure they offer a wide range of insurance products tailored to your needs.

- Reputation: Check references, reviews, and professional affiliations to verify their credibility.

- Customer Service: Choose an agent who

provides excellent customer service and clear communication.

Mentor or Real Estate Coach

A mentor or real estate coach provides guidance, support, and advice based on their experience and expertise in the industry.

Roles and Responsibilities:

- Guidance and Advice: Mentors offer insights and advice on real estate investing strategies, market trends, and best practices.

- Networking Opportunities: They introduce you to valuable contacts and resources within the real estate industry.

- Accountability: Mentors help you set goals, track progress, and stay accountable to your investment plans.

- Education and Training: They provide education and training on various aspects of real estate investing, from property acquisition to management.

Choosing the Right Mentor or Coach:

- Experience: Look for mentors with extensive experience and a successful track record in real estate investing.

- Compatibility: Choose a mentor whose

- investment philosophy and approach align with your goals.

- Reputation: Check references, reviews, and testimonials to ensure they have a positive reputation.

- Commitment: Ensure the mentor is committed to your success and willing to invest time and effort in your development.

Building a strong real estate team is essential for navigating the complexities of real estate investing and achieving long-term success. By assembling a team of experienced and reliable professionals, you can leverage their expertise to make informed decisions, manage properties effectively, and maximize returns. Each team member plays a crucial role in supporting your investment journey, from acquisition to management and beyond.

Creating an Investment Plan: Setting Up for Success

Creating a comprehensive investment plan is a critical step in setting yourself up for success in real estate investing. An investment plan provides a roadmap for achieving your financial goals, guiding your decision-making process, and ensuring you stay focused and organized. This section will explore the key components of an effective investment plan, including goal setting, market analysis, financing strategies, property selection, risk management, and performance evaluation.

Setting Investment Goals

The first step in creating an investment plan is to set clear and specific investment goals. These goals will guide your strategy and help you measure your progress.

Defining Your Objectives:

- Financial Goals: Determine your financial objectives, such as generating passive income, achieving capital appreciation, or building long-term wealth. Quantify these goals in terms of desired income levels, net worth targets, or return on investment (ROI).

- Time Horizon: Establish a timeline for achieving your goals. Are you looking for short-term gains or long-term growth? Define your investment horizon to align your strategy with your goals.

- Risk Tolerance: Assess your risk tolerance to determine the types of investments that suit your comfort level. Consider factors such as market volatility, economic cycles, and personal financial stability.

- Lifestyle Goals: Consider how real estate investing fits into your overall lifestyle and career goals. Are you seeking financial independence, early retirement, or a flexible work-life balance?

Setting SMART Goals:

- Specific: Clearly define your goals with specific details. For example, "Acquire three rental properties within the next two years."

- Measurable: Ensure your goals are measurable so you can track your progress. For example, "Generate $5,000 in monthly rental income within five years."

- Achievable: Set realistic goals that are attainable based on your resources, market conditions, and expertise.

- Relevant: Ensure your goals align with your overall investment strategy and long-term vision.

- Time-Bound: Establish deadlines for achieving your goals to create a sense of urgency and accountability.

Conducting Market Analysis

Market analysis is essential for identifying investment opportunities and assessing the viability of your investment plan. Understanding market trends, property values, and rental demand helps you make informed decisions.

Researching Target Markets:

- Economic Indicators: Analyze economic indicators such as GDP growth, employment rates, income levels, and population growth. Strong economic fundamentals indicate a healthy market with potential for appreciation.

- Real Estate Trends: Monitor real estate trends, including median home prices, rental rates, vacancy rates, and days on market. These trends provide insights into supply and demand dynamics.

- Demographic Data: Study demographic data, such as age distribution, household composition, and migration patterns. Understanding the demographics of your target market helps you tailor your property offerings to meet demand.

- Local Regulations: Familiarize yourself with local regulations, zoning laws, and property taxes. Compliance with local regulations is crucial for successful real estate investing.

Comparative Market Analysis (CMA):

- Identifying Comparable Properties: Identify properties similar to your target property in terms of location, size, condition, and amenities. These comparable properties (comps) provide a benchmark for assessing property values and rental rates.

- Analyzing Sales and Rental Data: Analyze recent sales and rental data for comparable properties to determine market value and rental income potential. Look for trends in pricing, days on market, and rental rates to gauge market conditions.

- Adjusting for Differences: Adjust the data for differences between the subject property and comparable properties. Consider factors such as property condition, upgrades, and unique features that may impact value and rental income.

Developing Financing Strategies

Securing financing is a critical component of your investment plan. Understanding the different financing options and developing a strategy that aligns with your goals is essential for success.

Exploring Financing Options:

- Conventional Mortgages: Traditional mortgages offered by banks and credit unions with fixed or adjustable interest rates. Suitable for residential properties and investors with good credit.

- FHA and VA Loans: Government-backed loans for first-time homebuyers (FHA) or veterans (VA) with favorable terms and lower down payment requirements.

- Commercial Loans: Loans for commercial properties with different terms and requirements compared to residential mortgages. Suitable for office buildings, retail spaces, and multifamily units.

- Private Lenders: Private lenders offer flexible financing options with shorter approval times but may have higher interest rates. Suitable for fix-and-flip projects and short-term investments.

- Hard Money Loans: Short-term loans secured by real estate, often used for renovation projects. Suitable for investors who need quick access to funds and are willing to pay higher interest rates.

Calculating Financing Costs:

- Interest Rates: Compare interest rates from different lenders to find the most favorable terms. Lower interest rates reduce your borrowing costs and increase your cash flow.

- Loan Terms: Consider the loan terms, including the repayment period, prepayment penalties, and amortization schedule. Longer loan terms may offer lower monthly payments but higher overall interest costs.

- Down Payment: Determine the down payment required for your financing option. Higher down payments reduce your loan amount and monthly payments but require more upfront capital.

- Closing Costs: Account for closing costs, including appraisal fees, inspection fees, title insurance, and legal fees. These costs can add up and impact your overall budget.

- Creating a Financing Plan:

- Budgeting for Financing: Create a budget that includes your financing costs, down payment, and closing costs. Ensure you have sufficient funds to cover these expenses without compromising your cash flow.

- Securing Pre-Approval: Obtain pre-approval from your lender to strengthen your position as a buyer and expedite the acquisition process.

- Exploring Creative Financing: Consider creative financing options, such as seller financing, lease options, and partnerships, to leverage other people's resources and minimize your upfront capital.

Selecting the Right Properties

Choosing the right properties is crucial for achieving your investment goals and maximizing returns. Consider factors such as location, property type, condition, and potential for appreciation and cash flow.

Evaluating Property Location:

- Neighborhood Analysis: Assess the quality of the neighborhood, including safety, amenities, schools, and transportation. Desirable neighborhoods attract quality tenants and offer potential for appreciation.

- Proximity to Employment Centers: Properties located near employment centers, business districts, and industrial hubs tend to have higher rental demand and lower vacancy rates.

- Future Development: Consider the impact of future development and infrastructure projects on property values. Areas with planned developments and improved transportation can experience significant appreciation.

- Market Trends: Analyze local market trends, including rental rates, vacancy rates, and property values. Target markets with positive trends and growth potential.

Assessing Property Condition:

- Property Inspection: Conduct a thorough property inspection to assess the condition of the property. Identify any structural issues, necessary repairs, and potential upgrades.
- Renovation Potential: Evaluate the potential for renovations and value-add improvements. Properties with the potential for upgrades can offer higher returns through forced appreciation.

- Maintenance Requirements: Consider the ongoing maintenance requirements of the property. Properties with high maintenance needs may impact your cash flow and profitability.

Analyzing Cash Flow and ROI:

- Rental Income: Estimate the potential rental income based on market rates and comparable properties. Ensure the rental income covers your operating expenses, financing costs, and desired cash flow.

- Operating Expenses: Calculate the operating expenses, including property taxes, insurance, maintenance, property management fees, and utilities. Factor in reserves for vacancies and unexpected repairs.

- Net Operating Income (NOI): Determine the Net Operating Income by subtracting operating expenses from rental income. NOI provides a clear picture of the property's profitability.

- Return on Investment (ROI): Calculate the ROI by dividing the annual cash flow by the total investment (purchase price plus financing costs). Aim for properties with a positive ROI that meets your investment goals.

Implementing Risk Management Strategies

Risk management is essential for protecting your investments and ensuring long-term success. Identifying potential risks and developing strategies to mitigate them is crucial for a resilient investment plan.

Diversifying Your Portfolio:

- Property Types: Diversify your portfolio by investing in different property types, including residential, commercial, and multifamily properties. Diversification reduces reliance on a single income stream and spreads risk.

- Geographic Locations: Invest in properties across different geographic locations to mitigate regional risks. Diversifying across multiple markets reduces exposure to local economic downturns and market fluctuations.

- Market Segments: Consider investing in niche markets, such as student housing, senior living, or vacation rentals. Niche markets offer unique opportunities and can enhance portfolio resilience.

Obtaining Insurance Coverage:

- Property Insurance: Secure property insurance to protect against physical damage, natural disasters, and other risks. Ensure the coverage amount reflects the property's value and potential repair costs.

- Liability Insurance: Obtain liability insurance to protect against legal claims and potential liabilities. Liability coverage is essential for rental properties to safeguard against tenant-related claims.

- Landlord Insurance: Landlord insurance

provides coverage for rental income loss, tenant-related damages, and legal expenses. This specialized coverage protects your rental income and reduces financial risks.

Conducting Due Diligence:

- Property Inspections: Conduct thorough property inspections to identify potential issues and assess the property's condition. Addressing issues upfront reduces the risk of unexpected repairs and expenses.

- Title Search: Perform a title search to ensure the property has a clear title, free of liens or legal disputes. Clear title ensures smooth ownership transfer and protects against future claims.

- Market Analysis: Conduct comprehensive market analysis to understand market conditions, rental demand, and property values. Accurate market data helps you make informed investment decisions.

Establishing Financial Reserves:

- Emergency Fund: Set aside an emergency fund to cover unexpected expenses, vacancies, and economic downturns. Having financial reserves provides a cushion to navigate challenges without compromising cash flow.

- Maintenance Reserves: Allocate reserves for routine maintenance and repairs. Proactive maintenance reduces the risk of major repairs and enhances tenant satisfaction.

- Vacancy Reserves: Establish reserves to cover potential vacancies and tenant turnover. Vacancy reserves ensure you can meet financial obligations during periods of low occupancy.

Evaluating Performance and Adjusting the Plan

Regularly evaluating the performance of your investments and adjusting your plan as needed is essential for long-term success. Continuous monitoring and adaptation help you stay on track and achieve your investment goals.

Tracking Key Performance Indicators (KPIs):

- Cash Flow: Monitor the cash flow from your properties, including rental income, operating expenses, and net income. Positive cash flow ensures financial stability and supports growth.

- Occupancy Rates: Track occupancy rates to assess tenant retention and rental demand. High occupancy rates indicate strong rental demand and effective property management.

- Property Value: Regularly assess property values to gauge appreciation and equity growth. Property value appreciation enhances your net worth and potential returns.

- ROI and Cap Rate: Calculate ROI and cap rate

to evaluate the profitability of your investments. Aim for properties with strong ROI and competitive cap rates.

Conducting Regular Reviews:

- Quarterly Reviews: Conduct quarterly reviews to assess the performance of your investments and track progress towards your goals. Quarterly reviews provide timely insights and allow for proactive adjustments.

- Annual Reviews: Perform annual reviews to evaluate the overall performance of your portfolio and refine your investment strategy. Annual reviews provide a comprehensive view of your progress and long-term goals.

- Adjusting the Plan: Based on your reviews, adjust your investment plan as needed to stay on track. Consider market conditions, economic trends, and personal circumstances when making adjustments.

Continuous Learning and Improvement:

- Education and Training: Invest in your education and stay updated with industry trends, market conditions, and best practices. Continuous learning enhances your knowledge and decision-making skills.

- Networking and Mentorship: Network with other investors and seek mentorship from experienced professionals. Networking provides valuable insights, support, and opportunities for collaboration.

- Adaptability: Stay adaptable and open to new opportunities and challenges. Real estate markets are dynamic, and flexibility is key to navigating changing conditions.

Creating a comprehensive investment plan is essential for setting yourself up for success in real estate investing. By setting clear investment goals, conducting market analysis, developing financing strategies, selecting the right properties, implementing risk management strategies, and regularly evaluating performance, you can achieve your financial objectives and build a successful real estate portfolio. An effective investment plan provides a roadmap for achieving your goals, guiding your decision-making process, and ensuring you stay focused and organized. With careful planning, strategic execution, and continuous improvement, you can navigate the complexities of real estate investing and achieve long-term success.

Chapter 3

Financial Planning and Budgeting

Financial planning and budgeting are crucial components of successful real estate investing. They provide a structured approach to managing your finances, ensuring you have the necessary resources to acquire and maintain properties, and optimizing your investment returns. This section will explore the various aspects of financial planning and budgeting, with a focus on securing financing and understanding different types of loans and mortgages.

Securing Financing: Different Types of Loans and Mortgages

Securing financing is one of the first and most important steps in real estate investing. The type of financing you choose can significantly impact your investment strategy, cash flow, and overall returns. Here, we will explore the different types of loans and mortgages available to real estate investors, highlighting their benefits, drawbacks, and suitability for various investment scenarios.

Conventional Mortgages

Conventional mortgages are the most common type of financing for residential real estate investments.

These loans are not insured or guaranteed by the federal government and are offered by private lenders, such as banks, credit unions, and mortgage companies.

Benefits:

- Lower Interest Rates: Conventional mortgages typically offer lower interest rates compared to other loan types, especially for borrowers with good credit.

- Flexible Terms: These loans come with various term options, ranging from 10 to 30 years, allowing borrowers to choose a repayment period that suits their financial goals.

- No Mortgage Insurance Requirement: If you make a down payment of 20% or more, you can avoid private mortgage insurance (PMI), which reduces your monthly payment.

Drawbacks:

- Stricter Qualification Criteria: Conventional mortgages have stricter qualification criteria, including higher credit score requirements and lower debt-to-income (DTI) ratios.

- Higher Down Payment: These loans typically require a down payment of at least 20%, which can be a significant barrier for some investors.

- Income Verification: Lenders require thorough income verification, including tax returns, pay stubs, and bank statements, which can be cumbersome for self-employed borrowers.

Suitability:

Conventional mortgages are suitable for investors with strong credit scores, stable incomes, and substantial down payment savings. They are ideal for purchasing single-family homes, duplexes, and smaller multi-family properties.

FHA Loans

Federal Housing Administration (FHA) loans are government-insured loans designed to help first-time homebuyers and individuals with lower credit scores and smaller down payments.

Benefits:

- Lower Down Payment: FHA loans require a down payment as low as 3.5%, making them more accessible for investors with limited capital.

- Lenient Credit Requirements: These loans have more lenient credit score requirements, allowing borrowers with lower credit scores to qualify.

- Assumable Loans: FHA loans are assumable, meaning a new buyer can take over the existing loan under the same terms, which can be an attractive feature in a rising interest rate environment.

Drawbacks:

- Mortgage Insurance Premiums (MIP): FHA loans require both an upfront mortgage insurance premium (UFMIP) and annual mortgage insurance premiums (MIP), which increase the overall cost of the loan.

- Loan Limits: There are limits on the amount you can borrow with an FHA loan, which may not be sufficient for higher-priced properties or larger investments.

- Primary Residence Requirement: FHA loans are intended for primary residences, but they can be used for multi-family properties (up to four units) if the borrower occupies one of the units.

Suitability:

FHA loans are suitable for first-time investors, those with lower credit scores, and those with limited funds for a down payment. They are ideal for purchasing multi-family properties where the investor plans to live in one unit.

VA Loans

Veterans Affairs (VA) loans are government-backed loans available to veterans, active-duty service members, and eligible spouses. These loans offer favorable terms and benefits as a reward for military service.

Benefits:

- No Down Payment: VA loans offer 100% financing, meaning eligible borrowers can purchase properties with no down payment.

- No Private Mortgage Insurance (PMI): VA loans do not require PMI, reducing the overall cost of the loan.

- Competitive Interest Rates: These loans typically offer lower interest rates compared to conventional mortgages.

- Flexible Credit Requirements: VA loans have more flexible credit score requirements, making them accessible to a broader range of borrowers.

Drawbacks:

- Funding Fee: VA loans require a funding fee, which can be financed into the loan or paid upfront. The fee varies based on the loan amount, type of service, and down payment.

- Primary Residence Requirement: VA loans are intended for primary residences, but they can be used for multi-family properties (up to four units) if the borrower occupies one of the units.

- Property Condition Requirements: VA appraisals have strict property condition requirements, which can be a barrier when purchasing fixer-uppers or properties in need of significant repairs.

Suitability:

VA loans are ideal for eligible veterans, active-duty service members, and their families. They are particularly beneficial for those with limited savings for a down payment and those looking to invest in multi-family properties while occupying one of the units.

USDA Loans

United States Department of Agriculture (USDA) loans are government-backed loans designed to help individuals in rural and suburban areas purchase homes with no down payment.

Benefits:

- No Down Payment: USDA loans offer 100% financing, allowing borrowers to purchase properties with no down payment.

- Low Mortgage Insurance Rates: These loans have lower mortgage insurance rates compared to FHA loans.

- Competitive Interest Rates: USDA loans offer competitive interest rates, making them an affordable financing option.

Drawbacks:

- Geographic Restrictions: USDA loans are only

available in eligible rural and suburban areas, which may limit your property choices.

- Income Limits: There are income limits for USDA loans, which may disqualify higher-income borrowers.

- Primary Residence Requirement: USDA loans are intended for primary residences and cannot be used for investment properties or vacation homes.

Suitability:

USDA loans are suitable for investors looking to purchase properties in rural or suburban areas and those with limited funds for a down payment. They are ideal for buyers who meet the income and geographic eligibility requirements.

Commercial Real Estate Loans

Commercial real estate loans are designed for purchasing income-producing properties, such as office buildings, retail centers, industrial properties, and multi-family apartment complexes.

Benefits:

- Higher Loan Amounts: Commercial loans offer higher loan amounts compared to residential mortgages, making them suitable for larger investments.

- Flexible Terms: These loans come with flexible

terms and structures, including fixed-rate, adjustable-rate, and interest-only options.

- Income-Based Qualification: Lenders primarily assess the property's income potential and cash flow rather than the borrower's personal income.

Drawbacks:

- Higher Interest Rates: Commercial loans often come with higher interest rates compared to residential mortgages.

- Shorter Loan Terms: These loans typically have shorter repayment terms, ranging from 5 to 20 years.

- Larger Down Payment: Commercial loans usually require a larger down payment, often between 20% and 30% of the property's purchase price.

- Complex Qualification Process: The qualification process for commercial loans is more complex, involving detailed financial analysis and extensive documentation.

Suitability:

Commercial real estate loans are ideal for investors looking to purchase income-producing properties, such as office buildings, retail centers, and large multi-family complexes. They are suitable for experienced investors with substantial capital and a solid understanding of commercial real estate markets.

Hard Money Loans

Hard money loans are short-term, asset-based loans typically used by real estate investors for fix-and-flip projects or properties that do not qualify for traditional financing.

Benefits:

- Quick Approval and Funding: Hard money lenders can provide fast approval and funding, making them ideal for time-sensitive deals.

- Flexible Qualification: These loans are based on the property's value rather than the borrower's creditworthiness, making them accessible to investors with lower credit scores or unconventional financial situations.

- No Prepayment Penalties: Many hard money loans do not have prepayment penalties, allowing investors to repay the loan early without incurring additional costs.

Drawbacks:

- High Interest Rates: Hard money loans come with higher interest rates compared to traditional mortgages, reflecting the increased risk for lenders.

- Short-Term Nature: These loans typically have

short repayment terms, ranging from 6 months to 3 years, requiring quick property turnover or refinancing.

- High Fees: Hard money loans often include high origination fees, points, and closing costs, increasing the overall cost of borrowing.

Suitability:

Hard money loans are suitable for experienced investors engaged in fix-and-flip projects or those needing quick financing for time-sensitive deals. They are ideal for properties that require significant renovations or do not qualify for traditional financing.

Private Money Loans

Private money loans are similar to hard money loans but are provided by private individuals or investors rather than professional lending institutions.

Benefits:

- Flexibility: Private money lenders can offer flexible terms and conditions tailored to the borrower's needs.

- Quick Approval and Funding: These loans can be approved and funded quickly, making them suitable for time-sensitive deals.

- Relationship-Based: Private money loans are often based on personal relationships and trust, which can lead to more favorable terms.

Drawbacks:

- Higher Interest Rates: Private money loans typically come with higher interest rates compared to traditional mortgages.

- Short-Term Nature: These loans are usually short-term, requiring quick property turnover or refinancing.

- Limited Availability: Finding private money lenders can be challenging, and the availability of funds may be limited.

Suitability:

Private money loans are suitable for investors with strong personal networks and those needing quick financing for time-sensitive deals. They are ideal for fix-and-flip projects or properties that require significant renovations.

Home Equity Loans and Lines of Credit (HELOCs)

Home equity loans and lines of credit (HELOCs) allow investors to leverage the equity in their existing properties to finance new investments.

Benefits:

- Access to Capital: These loans provide access to capital based on the equity in your existing property, allowing you to finance new investments without selling the property.

- Lower Interest Rates: Home equity loans and HELOCs often have lower interest rates compared to other types of loans.

- Flexible Use of Funds: The funds can be used for various purposes, including property acquisition, renovations, or other investment needs.

Drawbacks:

- Risk of Foreclosure: Using your property as collateral puts it at risk of foreclosure if you default on the loan.

- Variable Interest Rates: HELOCs often have variable interest rates, which can increase over time and impact your cash flow.

- Limited Loan Amount: The loan amount is limited to the available equity in your property, which may not be sufficient for larger investments.

Suitability:

Home equity loans and HELOCs are suitable for investors with significant equity in their existing properties and those looking to finance new investments without selling their assets. They are ideal for financing property acquisitions, renovations, or other investment needs.

Creating a Financing Strategy

Creating a financing strategy involves selecting the right type of loan for your investment goals, understanding the costs associated with financing, and preparing the necessary documentation for loan applications.

Assessing Your Financial Situation:

- Credit Score: Review your credit score and take steps to improve it if necessary. A higher credit score can help you qualify for better loan terms and lower interest rates.

- Income and Expenses: Analyze your income and expenses to determine your ability to make mortgage payments and cover other investment-related costs.

- Debt-to-Income Ratio: Calculate your debt-to-income (DTI) ratio to ensure it meets the lender's requirements. A lower DTI ratio improves your chances of loan approval.

Choosing the Right Loan Type:

- Investment Goals: Consider your investment goals, such as generating rental income, achieving capital appreciation, or flipping properties. Choose a loan type that aligns with your strategy.

- Loan Terms: Evaluate the loan terms, including interest rates, repayment periods, and fees.

Choose a loan that offers favorable terms and fits your financial situation.

- Property Type: Consider the type of property you are investing in and select a loan type suitable for that property. Different loans are designed for residential, commercial, or multi-family properties.

Preparing for the Loan Application:

- Documentation: Gather the necessary documentation for the loan application, including tax returns, pay stubs, bank statements, and property information. Ensure all documents are accurate and up-to-date.

- Pre-Approval: Obtain pre-approval from your lender to strengthen your position as a buyer and expedite the acquisition process.

- Financial Plan: Create a comprehensive financial plan that outlines your investment strategy, projected income, expenses, and cash flow. Presenting a solid financial plan can improve your chances of loan approval.

Securing financing is a critical step in real estate investing, and understanding the different types of loans and mortgages available is essential for making informed decisions. By assessing your financial situation, choosing the right loan type, and preparing for the loan application process, you can secure the financing needed to achieve your investment goals. A well-planned financing strategy helps you optimize your investment returns, manage risks, and build a successful real estate portfolio.

Budgeting for Investment: Initial Costs and Reserves

Creating a comprehensive budget is crucial for successful real estate investing. A well-planned budget helps you understand the financial requirements of your investment, ensuring you have the necessary funds to cover initial costs and maintain financial stability. This section will explore the different types of initial costs associated with real estate investing, the importance of maintaining reserves, and strategies for effective budgeting.

Initial Costs

The initial costs of a real estate investment encompass all the expenses incurred from the moment you decide to purchase a property until the day you close the deal. These costs can be significant and vary depending on the type of property, its location, and the specifics of the deal. Understanding and accurately estimating these initial costs is essential for effective budgeting.

Down Payment

The down payment is a substantial portion of the initial costs and varies based on the type of financing you secure.

- Conventional Loans: Typically require a down payment of 20% of the property's purchase price. For example, if you're purchasing a property for $300,000, you would need to provide $60,000 as a down payment.

- FHA Loans: Require a lower down payment, often as low as 3.5%. On a $300,000 property, this would amount to $10,500.

- VA and USDA Loans: These loans often require no down payment, making them attractive options for eligible buyers.

Closing Costs

- Closing costs are fees paid at the end of a real estate transaction and can add up to 2-5% of the property's purchase price. These costs typically include:

- Loan Origination Fees: Charged by lenders for processing the loan application, these fees are usually around 1% of the loan amount.

- Appraisal Fees: An appraisal is required to determine the property's market value, typically costing $300 to $500.

- Title Insurance and Search Fees: These fees protect against legal issues related to the property's title and can range from $500 to $1,500.

- Inspection Fees: Home inspections ensure the property is in good condition and may cost $300 to $500.

- Attorney Fees: Legal fees for reviewing documents and overseeing the closing process, which can range from $500 to $1,500.

- Recording Fees: Fees paid to the local government to record the new ownership of the property, typically around $100 to $200.

- Prepaid Costs: These include property taxes, homeowner's insurance, and interest prepayments, which vary depending on the property's location and value.

Renovation and Repair Costs

If the property requires renovations or repairs before it can be rented out or sold, these costs must be included in your budget. These can vary widely based on the scope of work and the condition of the property.

- Cosmetic Repairs: Minor repairs such as painting, flooring, and landscaping, which can range from a few hundred to several thousand dollars.

- Major Renovations: Significant upgrades like kitchen or bathroom remodels, roof replacement, or structural repairs, which can cost tens of thousands of dollars.

- Contingency Fund: It's prudent to set aside a contingency fund of 10-20% of your renovation budget to cover unexpected costs that arise during the project.

- Marketing and Leasing Costs

To attract tenants or buyers, you may need to invest in marketing and leasing costs.

- Advertising: Costs for listing the property on real estate websites, social media, and local newspapers, which can range from $100 to $500.

- Staging: Professional staging to make the property more appealing to potential buyers, typically costing $1,000 to $3,000.

- Leasing Fees: Fees paid to a property management company or real estate agent to find and screen tenants, usually one month's rent or 6-10% of the annual rent.

Reserve Funds

Maintaining reserve funds is crucial for covering unexpected expenses and ensuring financial stability. These reserves act as a financial cushion, protecting you from unforeseen costs that could disrupt your cash flow.

- Emergency Fund: An emergency fund should cover 3-6 months of operating expenses, including mortgage payments, property taxes, insurance, and maintenance costs. This ensures you can manage unexpected vacancies, repairs, or economic downturns without financial strain.

- Maintenance Reserves: Regular maintenance is essential for preserving the value of your property and ensuring tenant satisfaction. Set aside 1-2% of the property's value annually for maintenance and repairs. For a $300,000 property, this would amount to $3,000 to $6,000 per year.

- Capital Expenditure Reserves: Capital expenditures (CapEx) are major expenses for long-term improvements or replacements, such as roof repairs, HVAC systems, or major appliances. Plan for these costs by setting aside funds based on the property's age and condition. For example, setting aside $500 to $1,000 per unit annually for multi-family properties.

- Vacancy Reserves: It's essential to plan for periods when the property may be vacant. Set aside 1-2 months' worth of rental income annually to cover potential vacancies. This ensures you can continue to meet your financial obligations even when the property is not generating income.

Effective Budgeting Strategies

Effective budgeting involves careful planning, accurate estimation, and ongoing monitoring of your finances. Here are some strategies to help you create and maintain a robust budget for your real estate investments:

- Detailed Planning: Create a comprehensive budget that includes all initial costs, ongoing expenses, and reserve funds. Break down each category to ensure no costs are overlooked.

- Accurate Estimation: Research and gather quotes for all expected costs, including down payment, closing costs, renovations, and marketing. Use conservative estimates to avoid underestimating expenses.

- Cash Flow Analysis: Perform a cash flow analysis to project your income and expenses over time. This helps you understand your financial position and plan for future investments.

- Regular Monitoring: Continuously monitor your budget and compare actual expenses to your estimates. Adjust your budget as needed to account for any changes or unexpected costs.

- Contingency Planning: Always include a contingency fund in your budget to cover unforeseen expenses. This provides a financial buffer and ensures you can handle unexpected challenges.

- Professional Assistance: Consider working with a financial advisor, accountant, or real estate consultant to help you create and manage your budget. Their expertise can provide valuable insights and ensure your budget is realistic and comprehensive.

Understanding Cash Flow: Income and Expenses

Cash flow is the lifeblood of real estate investing. It represents the net amount of cash being generated from your investment properties, which is crucial for covering expenses, reinvesting in additional properties, and achieving financial goals. This section will delve into the components of cash flow, including income and expenses, and provide strategies for optimizing cash flow to maximize returns.

Income Sources

Understanding the various sources of income from your real estate investments is essential for accurate cash flow analysis. The primary sources of income include rental income, ancillary income, and appreciation.

Rental Income

Rental income is the most significant source of cash flow for real estate investors. It includes the monthly rent payments received from tenants.

- Gross Rental Income: This is the total income generated from rental payments before any expenses are deducted. For example, if you have three rental units each paying $1,500 per month, your gross rental income would be $4,500 per month or $54,000 annually.

- Rent Increases: Over time, you can increase

rental income by raising rents. Ensure rent increases comply with local regulations and market conditions. Regularly reviewing and adjusting rental rates can help maximize your rental income.

- Lease Agreements: Well-structured lease agreements ensure consistent rental income and protect against tenant defaults. Include clauses for rent payment schedules, late fees, and lease termination conditions.

Ancillary Income

Ancillary income refers to additional income generated from services or amenities provided to tenants. This can significantly boost your overall cash flow.

- Laundry Facilities: If your property has on-site laundry facilities, you can charge tenants for using these services. For example, charging $2 per load can generate extra income if multiple tenants use the facility.

- Parking Fees: Charging for parking spaces, especially in high-demand areas, can provide additional income. For instance, charging $50 per month for a parking space can add up over time.

- Storage Units: Offering storage units or lockers for rent can generate ancillary income. Charging $30 to $50 per month per unit can significantly boost your cash flow.

- Pet Fees: Charging pet fees or pet rent for tenants with pets can provide extra income. For example, a one-time pet fee of $300 or monthly pet rent of $25 can add up.

- Late Fees: Implementing late fees for overdue rent payments can encourage timely payments and generate additional income. Charging a $50 late fee after a grace period can incentivize tenants to pay on time.

Appreciation

While appreciation is not a direct source of cash flow, it contributes to the overall return on investment by increasing the property's value over time.

- Market Appreciation: This occurs when property values increase due to favorable market conditions, such as economic growth, infrastructure development, and increased demand. Monitoring local market trends can help you identify properties with strong appreciation potential.

- Forced Appreciation: Investors can achieve forced appreciation by improving the property's condition through renovations and upgrades. Strategic improvements, such as modernizing kitchens and bathrooms, can increase the property's market value and rental income.

- Equity Buildup: As you pay down the

mortgage, your equity in the property increases. This equity can be leveraged for additional investments, refinancing, or as a financial cushion. Understanding the balance between loan repayment and property value growth is crucial for maximizing equity buildup.

Expense Categories

Accurately tracking and managing expenses is vital for maintaining positive cash flow. The primary expense categories include operating expenses, financing costs, capital expenditures, and taxes.

Operating Expenses

Operating expenses are the ongoing costs associated with managing and maintaining your property. These expenses can significantly impact your cash flow if not properly managed.

- Property Management Fees: If you hire a property management company, their fees typically range from 8-12% of the monthly rental income. For example, if your monthly rental income is $4,500 and the management fee is 10%, you would pay $450 per month.

- Maintenance and Repairs: Regular maintenance and repairs are essential for preserving the property's value and ensuring tenant satisfaction. Budget for routine maintenance, such as landscaping, cleaning, and minor repairs, as well as unexpected repairs. Setting aside 1-2% of the property's value annually for maintenance is a good practice.

- Utilities: Depending on the lease agreement, you may be responsible for paying utilities such as water, gas, electricity, and trash removal. Estimate these costs based on historical data and local rates.

- Insurance: Property insurance protects against physical damage, liability claims, and loss of rental income. Ensure you have adequate coverage and budget for the annual premiums.

- Property Taxes: Property taxes are a significant expense and vary based on the property's location and assessed value. Stay informed about local tax rates and budget for annual tax payments.

- Advertising and Leasing: Marketing your property to attract tenants involves costs such as online listings, signage, and leasing commissions. Budget for these expenses to ensure your property remains occupied.

Financing Costs

Financing costs are the expenses associated with securing and maintaining a mortgage or loan for your property. These costs can significantly impact your cash flow.

- Mortgage Payments: Your monthly mortgage

payment typically includes principal and interest. Ensure you budget for these payments and monitor interest rate trends to anticipate any changes in your payment amounts.

- Private Mortgage Insurance (PMI): If your down payment is less than 20%, you may be required to pay PMI, which adds to your monthly mortgage payment. Budget for this additional cost if applicable.

- Loan Origination Fees: These are fees charged by lenders for processing your loan application and can be a significant upfront cost. Factor these fees into your initial budget.

- Refinancing Costs: If you decide to refinance your mortgage to secure better terms or lower interest rates, budget for the associated costs, including appraisal fees, closing costs, and any prepayment penalties.

Capital Expenditures (CapEx)

Capital expenditures are significant investments in long-term improvements or replacements that enhance the property's value and functionality.

- Major Repairs and Replacements: Budget for major repairs and replacements, such as roof repairs, HVAC system replacements, and plumbing upgrades. These costs can be substantial, so setting aside funds annually is essential.

- Renovations and Upgrades: Strategic renovations and upgrades, such as kitchen remodels, bathroom updates, and energy-efficient improvements, can increase the property's value and rental income. Plan for these projects and budget accordingly.

- Building Improvements: Investing in building improvements, such as landscaping, security systems, and common area enhancements, can attract higher-quality tenants and increase rental rates. Include these costs in your long-term budget.

Taxes

Taxes are an unavoidable expense for real estate investors, but understanding and managing your tax obligations can help minimize their impact on your cash flow.

- Property Taxes: As mentioned earlier, property taxes are a significant expense and vary by location. Stay informed about local tax rates and budget for annual payments.

- Income Taxes: Rental income is subject to federal and state income taxes. Work with a tax professional to understand your tax obligations and take advantage of deductions and credits.

- Capital Gains Taxes: If you sell a property for a profit, you may be subject to capital gains taxes. Planning for these taxes and exploring strategies like 1031 exchanges can help minimize their impact.

- Depreciation: Depreciation is a valuable tax deduction that allows you to offset rental income with the property's wear and tear over time. Understanding how to calculate and apply depreciation can significantly reduce your taxable income.

Optimizing Cash Flow

Optimizing cash flow involves maximizing income and minimizing expenses to ensure your real estate investment remains profitable. Here are some strategies to help you achieve positive cash flow:

Maximizing Rental Income

- Market Research: Conduct thorough market research to determine competitive rental rates in your area. Setting the right rental price ensures your property remains attractive to tenants while maximizing income.

- Lease Renewals: Encourage lease renewals by offering incentives to long-term tenants, such as rent discounts or upgrades. Retaining tenants reduces turnover costs and maintains a steady income stream.

- Regular Rent Increases: Implement regular rent increases to keep up with inflation and market conditions. Ensure increases comply with local regulations and are communicated clearly to tenants.

- Adding Amenities: Adding desirable amenities, such as in-unit laundry, upgraded appliances, or outdoor spaces, can justify higher rental rates and attract quality tenants.

Reducing Operating Expenses

- Energy Efficiency: Invest in energy-efficient upgrades, such as LED lighting, programmable thermostats, and energy-efficient appliances. These improvements can reduce utility costs and attract environmentally conscious tenants.

- Preventative Maintenance: Implement a preventative maintenance schedule to address minor issues before they become major problems. Regular maintenance can extend the lifespan of your property and reduce repair costs.

- Vendor Relationships: Establish relationships with reliable vendors and contractors to negotiate better rates for maintenance and repairs. Building long-term partnerships can result in cost savings and higher-quality work.

- Property Management: If you manage the property yourself, consider hiring a property management company to handle day-to-day operations. While this incurs a cost, professional management can improve efficiency and tenant satisfaction, ultimately enhancing cash flow.

Managing Financing Costs

- Refinancing: Monitor interest rate trends and consider refinancing your mortgage to secure lower rates or better terms. Refinancing can reduce your monthly payments and improve cash flow.

- Paying Down Principal: If you have extra funds, consider making additional principal payments to reduce your mortgage balance and interest costs over time. This strategy can enhance equity and lower financing expenses.

- Avoiding PMI: If possible, make a larger down payment to avoid private mortgage insurance (PMI). Eliminating PMI reduces your monthly payment and improves cash flow.

- Loan Shopping: Shop around for the best mortgage rates and terms before securing financing. Comparing offers from multiple lenders can result in better deals and lower financing costs.

Planning for Taxes

- Tax Deductions: Take advantage of tax deductions for mortgage interest, property taxes, maintenance, repairs, and depreciation. Work with a tax professional to ensure you're maximizing your deductions.

- 1031 Exchanges: Consider using a 1031 exchange to defer capital gains taxes when selling a property and reinvesting the proceeds into a similar property. This strategy can preserve your capital and enhance your investment portfolio.

- Depreciation: Understand how to calculate and apply depreciation to offset rental income. Properly accounting for depreciation can significantly reduce your taxable income.

- Tax Planning: Engage in proactive tax planning with a qualified tax advisor to develop strategies that minimize your tax liability and optimize your after-tax returns.

Financial planning and budgeting are critical components of successful real estate investing. By accurately estimating initial costs, maintaining reserves, understanding cash flow, and implementing strategies to optimize income and reduce expenses, you can achieve positive cash flow and maximize returns. A comprehensive budget and effective cash flow management provide a solid foundation for long-term financial stability and growth in your real estate investment journey. With careful planning, disciplined budgeting, and ongoing monitoring, you can navigate the complexities of real estate investing and achieve your financial goals.

Credit and Financing Strategies: Maximizing Your Borrowing Power

Credit and financing are fundamental components of real estate investing. The ability to secure favorable financing terms can significantly impact your investment returns and overall financial health. This section will explore various strategies to maximize your borrowing power, including understanding your credit score, improving your creditworthiness, and leveraging different financing options.

Understanding Your Credit Score

Your credit score is a critical factor that lenders consider when determining your eligibility for loans and the interest rates you will be offered. Here's what you need to know about credit scores:

Components of a Credit Score:

- Payment History (35%): Your history of on-time payments is the most significant factor affecting your credit score. Late payments, defaults, and collections can severely impact your score.

- Amounts Owed (30%): This factor considers your credit utilization ratio, which is the amount of credit you are using relative to your total credit limit. Lower utilization rates are better for your score.

- Length of Credit History (15%): The longer your credit history, the better. This includes the age of your oldest account, the age of your newest account, and the average age of all your accounts.

- Credit Mix (10%): A diverse mix of credit types (e.g., credit cards, mortgages, auto loans) can positively impact your score.

- New Credit (10%): Opening several new credit accounts in a short period can be seen as risky behavior and can negatively impact your score.

Improving Your Credit Score:

- Pay Bills on Time: Consistently making on-time payments is crucial. Set up automatic payments or reminders to ensure you never miss a due date.

- Reduce Debt: Pay down existing debt to lower your credit utilization ratio. Aim to keep your utilization below 30%.

- Avoid Opening New Accounts Unnecessarily: Each hard inquiry can slightly lower your score. Only apply for new credit when necessary.

- Check Your Credit Report: Regularly review your credit report for errors and dispute any inaccuracies with the credit bureaus.

Improving Your Creditworthiness

Improving your creditworthiness goes beyond your credit score. It involves demonstrating financial responsibility and stability to lenders. Here are some strategies:

Build a Strong Financial Profile:

- Maintain Steady Employment: Stable

employment history shows lenders that you have a reliable income source to repay loans.

- Increase Income: Higher income can improve your debt-to-income (DTI) ratio, making you a more attractive borrower. Consider additional income sources or side jobs.

- Manage Your Debt-to-Income Ratio: Aim to keep your DTI ratio below 36%, with no more than 28% of your gross monthly income going toward housing expenses.

Establish Relationships with Lenders:

- Cultivate Relationships: Build relationships with local banks and credit unions. They may offer more personalized service and favorable terms based on your history with them.

- Use Secured Credit Cards: If you have poor credit, using secured credit cards responsibly can help rebuild your credit history.

Leveraging Different Financing Options

Different financing options can provide flexibility and optimize your borrowing power. Here are several financing strategies to consider:

Traditional Mortgages:

- Fixed-Rate Mortgages: Offer stability with a fixed interest rate and monthly payment over the life of the loan. Suitable for long-term investments.

- Adjustable-Rate Mortgages (ARMs): Typically offer lower initial interest rates that adjust periodically. Suitable for short-term investments or if you expect interest rates to decrease.

Government-Backed Loans:

- FHA Loans: Require lower down payments and have more lenient credit requirements. Ideal for first-time investors or those with lower credit scores.

- VA Loans: Available to veterans and active-duty service members with no down payment and competitive interest rates.

- USDA Loans: Offer no down payment options for properties in eligible rural areas.

Portfolio Loans:

- Lender-Specific Loans: Held by the lender rather than being sold on the secondary market. These loans offer more flexibility in terms and conditions, making them suitable for investors with unique financial situations.

Hard Money Loans:

- Short-Term Financing: Secured by real estate, these loans are ideal for fix-and-flip projects or short-term investments. They offer quick approval but come with higher interest rates and fees.

Private Money Loans:

- Flexible Terms: These loans come from private individuals or groups and can be more flexible than traditional financing. Building a network of private lenders can provide access to capital for various investment opportunities.

Lines of Credit:

- Home Equity Line of Credit (HELOC): Allows you to borrow against the equity in your existing property. It's flexible and can be used for property improvements or new investments.

- Business Lines of Credit: Provide access to funds that can be used as needed, offering flexibility for property management or acquisition expenses.

Combining Financing Strategies

Combining different financing strategies can help you maximize your borrowing power and investment potential:

Cross-Collateralization:

- Using Multiple Properties: Leverage the equity in one property to secure a loan for another. This strategy can help you expand your portfolio without significant cash outlays.

Refinancing:

- Lower Interest Rates: Refinancing existing loans can lower your interest rates and monthly payments, freeing up cash for additional investments.

- Cash-Out Refinancing: Allows you to access the equity in your property for other investments. This can provide the funds needed for down payments or property improvements.

Seller Financing:

- Negotiating Terms: In seller financing, the seller acts as the lender, offering flexible terms that can benefit both parties. This can be particularly useful in competitive markets or for properties that are difficult to finance traditionally.

Real Estate Syndication:

- Pooling Resources: Join forces with other investors to purchase larger properties or projects. Syndication allows you to leverage the collective financial power of a group, increasing your investment potential.

Maximizing Borrowing Power with Strategic Planning

Effective planning and strategic use of credit and financing options can significantly enhance your borrowing power:

Pre-Approval:

- Strengthening Offers: Obtaining pre-approval from lenders can strengthen your offers and expedite the purchase process. It demonstrates to sellers that you are a serious and qualified buyer.

Negotiating Terms:

- Interest Rates and Fees: Always negotiate for better interest rates, lower fees, and favorable terms. Lenders may be willing to offer better deals to secure your business.

Utilizing Equity:

- Leveraging Existing Properties: Use the equity in your existing properties to secure financing for new investments. This can be done through HELOCs, cash-out refinancing, or cross-collateralization.

Continuous Monitoring:

- Credit Score: Regularly monitor your credit score and take proactive steps to maintain or improve it.
- Market Trends: Stay informed about market

trends and interest rates to time your financing decisions advantageously.

Maximizing your borrowing power involves a combination of understanding and improving your credit score, building a strong financial profile, and strategically leveraging various financing options. By employing these strategies, you can enhance your ability to secure favorable financing terms, expand your real estate portfolio, and achieve your investment goals.

Tax Planning: Deductions, Benefits, and Strategies

Effective tax planning is essential for real estate investors to maximize their returns and minimize their tax liabilities. Understanding the various deductions, benefits, and strategies available can significantly impact your financial outcomes. This section will explore the key aspects of tax planning for real estate investors, including common deductions, tax benefits, and strategic approaches to minimize taxes.

Common Deductions for Real Estate Investors

Real estate investors can take advantage of several tax deductions that can reduce their taxable income and enhance their overall returns. Here are some of the most common deductions:

Mortgage Interest:

- Deductible Interest: The interest paid on

mortgage loans for investment properties is tax-deductible. This can be a substantial deduction, especially in the early years of the mortgage when interest payments are higher.

Property Taxes:

- Local and State Taxes: Property taxes paid to local and state governments are deductible. This includes any special assessments levied for improvements or services.

Depreciation:

- Non-Cash Deduction: Depreciation allows you to deduct the cost of the property over its useful life. For residential properties, the depreciation period is 27.5 years, while for commercial properties, it is 39 years.

- Improvements and Renovations: Certain improvements and renovations can also be depreciated, reducing your taxable income further.

Operating Expenses:

- Maintenance and Repairs: Costs for routine maintenance and repairs are fully deductible in the year they are incurred. This includes expenses for cleaning, landscaping, and minor repairs.

- Property Management Fees: Fees paid to property management companies for managing your investment properties are deductible.

- Utilities: If you pay for utilities such as water, gas, and electricity, these expenses are deductible.

Travel Expenses:

- Property Management Travel: If you travel to manage your properties, the travel expenses, including mileage, lodging, and meals, can be deductible. Keep detailed records and receipts to substantiate these deductions.

Insurance Premiums:

- Property Insurance: Premiums paid for insurance coverage on your investment properties are deductible. This includes liability insurance, hazard insurance, and landlord insurance.

Professional Fees:

- Legal and Accounting Fees: Fees paid to attorneys, accountants, and other professionals for services related to your real estate investments are deductible. This includes fees for tax preparation, legal advice, and property management consultations.

Advertising and Marketing:

- Tenant Acquisition: Expenses incurred for

advertising and marketing your rental properties to attract tenants are deductible. This includes costs for online listings, print ads, and signage.

Tax Benefits for Real Estate Investors

In addition to deductions, Credit and Financing

Strategies: Maximizing Your Borrowing Power

Effective real estate investing hinges on your ability to secure favorable financing. Understanding how to maximize your borrowing power can significantly impact your investment strategy and returns. This section delves into credit and financing strategies to help you achieve this.

Understanding Your Credit Score

Your credit score is a crucial determinant of your borrowing capacity. It affects the interest rates you receive and the loan terms offered by lenders. Here are the primary components of a credit score:

- Payment History (35%): Timely payments on your debts are essential. Late payments, defaults, and collections can severely harm your score.

- Amounts Owed (30%): Your credit utilization ratio, which is the amount of credit you use compared to your credit limits, should ideally be below 30%.

- Length of Credit History (15%): The longer your credit accounts have been open, the better. This includes the age of your oldest and newest accounts and the average age of all your accounts.

- Credit Mix (10%): Having a mix of credit types (credit cards, mortgages, auto loans) can positively impact your score.

- New Credit (10%): Opening several new credit accounts in a short time can lower your score.

Improving Your Credit Score:

- Pay Bills on Time: Automate payments or set reminders to avoid late payments.

- Reduce Debt: Aim to lower your credit utilization ratio by paying down outstanding balances.

- Limit New Credit Applications: Only apply for new credit when necessary to avoid multiple hard inquiries.

- Regularly Check Credit Reports: Dispute any inaccuracies with credit bureaus to ensure your report is accurate.

Improving Your Creditworthiness

Improving your creditworthiness involves demonstrating financial responsibility beyond just your credit score. Here are strategies to enhance your financial profile:

- Stable Employment: A consistent employment history shows lenders that you have a reliable income to repay loans.

- Increase Income: Higher income improves your debt-to-income (DTI) ratio, making you more attractive to lenders. Explore additional income sources if possible.

- Manage Debt-to-Income Ratio: Keep your DTI ratio below 36%, with no more than 28% of your gross monthly income going towards housing expenses.

Building Relationships with Lenders:

- Local Banks and Credit Unions: Develop relationships with local financial institutions, which may offer more personalized service and better terms.

- Secured Credit Cards: Use secured credit cards to rebuild credit if you have a low credit score.

Leveraging Different Financing Options

Real estate investors have various financing options, each with distinct benefits and drawbacks.

Understanding and leveraging these options can maximize your borrowing power.

Traditional Mortgages:

- Fixed-Rate Mortgages: Offer stable interest rates and payments, suitable for long-term investments.

- Adjustable-Rate Mortgages (ARMs): Typically have lower initial rates that adjust periodically, suitable for short-term investments or if you expect interest rates to fall.

Government-Backed Loans:

- FHA Loans: Require low down payments and have lenient credit requirements, ideal for first-time investors.

- VA Loans: Available to veterans with no down payment and competitive interest rates.

- USDA Loans: Offer no down payment for properties in eligible rural areas.

Portfolio Loans:

- Lender-Specific Loans: These are not sold on the secondary market, offering flexibility in terms and conditions for investors with unique situations.

Hard Money Loans:

- Short-Term Financing: Secured by real estate, ideal for fix-and-flip projects. They offer quick approval but have higher interest rates and fees.

Private Money Loans:

- Flexible Terms: These loans come from private individuals or groups and can be more flexible than traditional financing.

Lines of Credit:

- Home Equity Line of Credit (HELOC): Borrow against the equity in your existing property. It's flexible and can be used for various investment needs.

- Business Lines of Credit: Provide funds as needed, offering flexibility for property management or acquisition expenses.

Combining Financing Strategies

Combining different financing strategies can optimize your borrowing power and investment potential:

Cross-Collateralization:

- Use equity in one property to secure a loan for another, expanding your portfolio without significant cash outlays.

- Refinancing:

- Refinance existing loans to lower interest rates and monthly payments, freeing up cash for additional investments.

- Cash-Out Refinancing: Access equity in your property for other investments, such as down payments or property improvements.

Seller Financing:

- Negotiate terms directly with the seller, which can be beneficial in competitive markets or for difficult-to-finance properties.

Real Estate Syndication:

- Pool resources with other investors to purchase larger properties or projects, leveraging collective financial power.

Strategic Planning for Maximizing Borrowing Power

Effective planning and strategic use of credit and financing options are crucial for maximizing your borrowing power:

Pre-Approval:

- Obtain pre-approval from lenders to strengthen your offers and expedite the purchase process.

Negotiating Terms:

- Always negotiate for better interest rates, lower fees, and favorable terms.

Utilizing Equity:

- Leverage the equity in your existing properties to secure financing for new investments through HELOCs, cash-out refinancing, or cross-collateralization.

Continuous Monitoring:

- Regularly monitor your credit score and market trends to time your financing decisions advantageously.

Chapter 4

Finding the Right Properties

Finding the right properties is a crucial step in building a successful real estate portfolio. This involves conducting thorough market research to identify promising areas and making informed decisions based on various factors. This section will explore strategies for market research and highlight key aspects to consider when identifying potential investment areas.

Market Research: Identifying Promising Areas

Effective market research is the foundation of successful real estate investing. By analyzing various market indicators and trends, you can identify areas with strong growth potential, high demand, and favorable investment conditions. Here are some strategies and factors to consider when conducting market research:

Analyzing Economic Indicators

Economic indicators provide valuable insights into the health and growth potential of a real estate market. Key indicators to consider include:

- Employment Rates:

- Job Growth: Areas with strong job growth tend to attract more residents, increasing demand for housing. Look for regions with a diverse and growing job market.

- Unemployment Rates: Low unemployment rates indicate a stable economy, which can lead to higher demand for rental properties and increased property values.

Income Levels:

- Median Household Income: Higher median incomes can signal greater purchasing power and the ability to afford higher rents. This is a positive indicator for rental property investors.

- Income Growth: Steady income growth over time suggests a robust economy and potential for property appreciation.

Population Growth:

- Migration Patterns: Analyze population trends, including migration patterns. Areas experiencing an influx of new residents are likely to have higher demand for housing.

- Demographics: Consider the age distribution and household composition. Young professionals, families, and retirees each have different housing needs and preferences.

Evaluating Real Estate Trends

Understanding real estate trends helps you gauge the supply and demand dynamics in a market. Key trends to analyze include:

- **Median Home Prices:**

    o Price Appreciation: Consistent appreciation in home prices indicates a healthy and growing market. Rapidly rising prices can also signal a potential for future gains.

    o Affordability: Ensure the market remains affordable for your target tenants or buyers. High prices may limit your potential tenant pool.

- **Rental Rates:**

    o Rental Yield: Calculate the rental yield (annual rental income divided by property price) to assess the profitability of rental properties. Higher yields indicate better returns.

    o Rental Demand: Look for areas with high rental demand, which can be indicated by low vacancy rates and a growing renter population.

- **Vacancy Rates:**

    o Low Vacancy Rates: Low vacancy rates

suggest strong rental demand and can lead to higher rental income and reduced risk of prolonged vacancies.

- Trends Over Time: Analyze how vacancy rates have changed over time. A decreasing vacancy rate is a positive sign of increasing demand.

- **Days on Market:**

  - Shorter Listing Periods: Properties that sell quickly indicate a strong seller's market and high demand. Conversely, longer listing periods may suggest weaker demand.

Assessing Local Amenities and Infrastructure

The availability of amenities and infrastructure plays a significant role in the desirability of an area. Consider the following factors:

- Proximity to Employment Centers:

  - Commuter Access: Areas close to major employment centers, business districts, and industrial hubs tend to have higher demand for housing.

- Transportation:

  - Public Transit: Access to reliable public transportation can increase the attractiveness of a location, particularly for renters.

- o Road Infrastructure: Good road connectivity and traffic conditions are essential for suburban and rural properties.

- Schools and Education:

    - o School Quality: Areas with highly-rated schools are often in demand among families, leading to higher property values and rental rates.

    - o Proximity to Educational Institutions: Proximity to colleges and universities can attract student renters and create a steady demand for rental properties.

- Healthcare Facilities:

    - o Hospital Access: Proximity to hospitals and healthcare facilities is a crucial consideration for many renters and buyers.

- Shopping and Entertainment:

    - o Retail and Dining: The availability of shopping centers, restaurants, and entertainment options enhances the desirability of an area.

    - o Recreational Facilities: Parks, gyms, and other recreational amenities contribute to the quality of life and attractiveness of a location.

- Studying Government Policies and Regulations

    o Government policies and regulations can significantly impact real estate markets. Stay informed about:

- Zoning Laws:

    o Development Opportunities: Understand local zoning laws to identify areas with development potential or restrictions that may affect property use.

- Tax Policies:

    o Property Taxes: Compare property tax rates across different areas. Lower taxes can improve cash flow and overall returns.

    o Incentives: Look for government incentives for real estate investment, such as tax abatements or grants for property improvements.

- Rent Control:

    o Regulations: Be aware of rent control regulations that may limit your ability to increase rents. While rent control can stabilize income, it may also cap potential returns.

- Future Infrastructure Projects:

  - Development Plans: Research planned infrastructure projects, such as new highways, public transit expansions, and commercial developments. These projects can enhance property values and demand.

- Utilizing Technology and Data Sources

  - Leverage technology and data sources to streamline your market research and make informed decisions:

- Real Estate Websites:

  - Listing Platforms: Use platforms like Zillow, Realtor.com, and Redfin to analyze property listings, prices, and market trends.

  - Market Reports: Access market reports and analysis provided by real estate websites and brokerage firms.

- Data Analytics Tools:

  - Neighborhood Analytics: Use tools like NeighborhoodScout and City-Data to gather detailed information on neighborhoods, including crime rates, school ratings, and demographic data.

- Rental Market Analysis: Utilize tools like Rentometer and Zillow's Rental Manager to compare rental rates and vacancy trends.

- GIS Mapping:

  - Geospatial Analysis: Geographic Information System (GIS) tools allow you to visualize data on maps, helping you identify patterns and trends in different areas.

- Public Records:

  - Property Records: Access public property records to gather information on property ownership, sales history, and tax assessments.

  - County and City Databases: Explore databases maintained by county and city governments for information on zoning, permits, and development plans.

- Networking and Local Insights

  - Building a network of local contacts can provide valuable insights and firsthand information about a market:

- Real Estate Agents:

  - Local Expertise: Partner with experienced local real estate agents who have deep knowledge of the market and can provide guidance on promising areas.

- o Off-Market Deals: Agents may have access to off-market properties and opportunities not listed publicly.

- Investors and Landlords:

    - o Peer Insights: Connect with other real estate investors and landlords to share experiences and gather insights on market conditions and investment opportunities.

    - o Investment Groups: Join local real estate investment groups or associations to expand your network and stay informed about market trends.

- Community Involvement:

    - o Local Events: Attend community events, town hall meetings, and planning commission hearings to stay informed about local developments and gain insights into the community.

- Property Managers:

    - o Operational Insights: Property managers can provide valuable information on rental demand, tenant preferences, and property management challenges in specific areas.

- Finding the right properties involves comprehensive market research and analysis. By evaluating economic indicators, real estate trends, local amenities, government policies, and utilizing technology and local insights, you can identify promising areas for investment. Thorough market research enables you to make informed decisions, minimize risks, and maximize returns on your real estate investments. With the right strategies and data-driven approach, you can build a successful and profitable real estate portfolio.

Property Search Methods: Online and Offline Strategies

Online Strategies

1. Real Estate Websites and Portals

The digital era has revolutionized how we search for real estate properties. Websites like Zillow, Realtor.com, and Redfin offer comprehensive listings with detailed information, photos, and even virtual tours. These platforms provide advanced search filters to narrow down properties by location, price range, size, and other specific features. Users can also set up alerts to receive notifications about new listings that match their criteria.

Advantages:

- Accessibility: You can access a vast number of

listings from the comfort of your home.

- Convenience: View multiple properties quickly without the need for physical visits.

- Comprehensive Data: Listings often include photos, videos, and detailed descriptions, giving a thorough initial overview.

Tips for Using Real Estate Websites:

- Set Up Alerts: To stay ahead of the competition, set up email alerts for new listings.

- Use Multiple Sites: Different sites might have unique listings, so broaden your search by using multiple platforms.

- Read Reviews: Some platforms offer reviews of neighborhoods or even specific buildings.

2. Social Media and Online Forums

Social media platforms like Facebook, Twitter, and Instagram have become valuable tools in the property search process. Many real estate agents and agencies maintain active profiles where they post about new listings and open houses. Additionally, online forums and groups, such as those on Reddit or Facebook, provide community insights and unlisted opportunities.

Advantages:

- Real-Time Updates: Social media can provide immediate information about new listings.

- Community Insights: Forums offer advice, reviews, and personal experiences from local residents.

- Networking: Directly connect with agents, sellers, and other buyers.

Tips for Using Social Media:

- Follow Local Real Estate Pages: Stay updated on the latest listings and market trends.

- Join Groups: Participate in real estate forums and groups to ask questions and get insider tips.

- Engage with Content: Comment on posts and ask questions to gather more information.

3. Real Estate Apps

Mobile applications like Zillow, Trulia, and Realtor.com have made property searching even more accessible. These apps offer the same functionalities as their website counterparts but with the added convenience of mobile accessibility. Features like map-based searches, neighborhood insights, and mortgage calculators enhance the user experience.

Advantages:

- On-the-Go Search: Search for properties anytime, anywhere.

- User-Friendly Interfaces: Intuitive designs make navigating listings easy.

- Personalized Recommendations: Apps often suggest properties based on previous searches and preferences.

Tips for Using Real Estate Apps:

- Enable Notifications: Get instant alerts for new listings and price changes.

- Use Map Features: Explore neighborhoods visually to get a better sense of the area.

- Explore Additional Tools: Utilize built-in mortgage calculators and neighborhood insights.

Offline Strategies

1. Real Estate Agents

Hiring a real estate agent remains one of the most effective ways to find properties. Agents have extensive knowledge of the local market and access to multiple listing services (MLS) that are not always available to the public. They can provide personalized service, negotiate deals, and guide you through the buying process.

Advantages:

- Expert Knowledge: Agents understand market trends, property values, and negotiation tactics.

- Exclusive Listings: Access to properties not listed online or still under development.

- Time-Saving: Agents can narrow down options and arrange viewings.

Tips for Working with Real Estate Agents:

- Choose a Local Expert: Ensure the agent has deep knowledge of the area you're interested in.

- Be Clear About Your Needs: Communicate your preferences and budget to your agent.

- Check References: Look for reviews or ask for references to gauge the agent's track record.

2. Open Houses and Property Tours

Attending open houses and property tours is a traditional yet effective method for evaluating properties. Open houses allow you to inspect the property firsthand, get a feel for the neighborhood, and ask questions directly to the seller or listing agent.

Advantages:

- Firsthand Experience: Physically inspect the

property and its surroundings.

- Immediate Feedback: Get answers to your questions on the spot.

- Meet Neighbors: Interact with current residents to learn about the community.

Tips for Attending Open Houses:

- Take Notes: Document your observations and any potential issues.

- Ask Questions: Inquire about the property's history, maintenance, and the seller's timeline.

- Observe the Neighborhood: Pay attention to nearby amenities, noise levels, and overall vibe.

3. Networking and Word of Mouth

Sometimes the best properties are discovered through personal connections and word of mouth. Friends, family, and colleagues can provide leads on properties before they hit the market. Networking with other real estate investors can also reveal opportunities that are not publicly listed.

Advantages:

- Early Access: Hear about properties before they are listed online.

- Trustworthy Recommendations: Leads from trusted sources are often more reliable.

- Building Relationships: Networking can open doors to future opportunities.

Tips for Networking:

- Attend Local Events: Real estate meetups and community events are great places to network.

- Leverage Social Networks: Use platforms like LinkedIn to connect with industry professionals.

- Keep in Touch: Maintain relationships with contacts who might provide leads in the future.

4. Driving Through Target Neighborhoods

Sometimes, driving through the neighborhoods you are interested in can reveal hidden gems. For Sale signs, construction sites, or areas undergoing revitalization might not be listed online yet. This method provides a real sense of the area's livability and potential growth.

Advantages:

- Discover Unlisted Properties: Find properties that aren't listed online.

- Assess Neighborhood Appeal: See the community's atmosphere and amenities firsthand.

- Spot Trends: Identify areas with increasing

development and potential appreciation.

Tips for Driving Through Neighborhoods:

- Plan Your Route: Focus on neighborhoods of interest and map out a route.

- Take Photos: Document properties and areas that catch your interest.

- Talk to Locals: Engage with residents to gather insights about the neighborhood.

Evaluating Properties: Key Criteria and Metrics

1. Location

The adage "location, location, location" holds true for real estate investment. A property's location significantly influences its value, rental potential, and future appreciation. Consider factors such as proximity to schools, transportation, shopping centers, and employment hubs.

Key Considerations:

- Neighborhood Quality: Assess the overall safety, cleanliness, and desirability of the neighborhood.

- School Districts: Properties in reputable school districts tend to have higher demand.

- Accessibility: Easy access to major roads,

public transportation, and amenities increases a property's attractiveness.

- Future Development: Investigate planned developments or infrastructure projects that could enhance the area's value.

2. Property Condition

The condition of a property affects both its current value and the cost of future maintenance and repairs. A thorough inspection can reveal potential issues such as structural problems, outdated systems, or cosmetic defects.

Key Considerations:

- Structural Integrity: Ensure the foundation, roof, and walls are in good condition.

- Systems and Utilities: Check the age and functionality of electrical, plumbing, heating, and cooling systems.

- Cosmetic Condition: Evaluate the interior and exterior finishes, fixtures, and overall aesthetic appeal.

- Pest and Mold Inspections: Look for signs of infestations or mold, which can lead to costly remediation.

3. Market Trends

Understanding current market trends helps in making

informed investment decisions. Analyze data on property values, rental rates, and vacancy rates to gauge the market's health and predict future performance.

Key Considerations:

- Price Trends: Review historical price data to identify patterns of appreciation or depreciation.

- Rental Rates: Compare rental rates in the area to assess potential rental income.

- Vacancy Rates: High vacancy rates may indicate low demand or oversupply, while low vacancy rates suggest strong demand.

- Economic Indicators: Monitor local economic conditions, employment rates, and population growth.

4. Financial Metrics

Evaluating the financial performance of a property involves analyzing various metrics to determine its profitability and potential return on investment (ROI).

Cash Flow

Cash flow is the net income generated from a rental property after deducting all expenses. Positive cash flow indicates that the property is generating more income than it costs to maintain.

Key Considerations:

- Gross Rental Income: Total income from rent before expenses.

- Operating Expenses: Costs associated with managing the property, including maintenance, utilities, property management fees, and insurance.

- Net Operating Income (NOI): Gross rental income minus operating expenses.

Cap Rate

The capitalization rate (cap rate) measures the expected rate of return on a real estate investment. It is calculated by dividing the NOI by the property's current market value.

Key Considerations:

- Formula: Cap Rate = (Net Operating Income / Current Market Value) x 100%

- Benchmarking: Compare the cap rate to similar properties in the area to assess competitiveness.

- Risk Assessment: Higher cap rates often indicate higher risk, while lower cap rates suggest lower risk and potentially higher stability.

ROI

Return on Investment (ROI) measures the profitability of an investment relative to its cost. It is calculated by dividing the net profit by the initial investment cost.

Key Considerations:

- Formula: ROI = (Net Profit / Initial Investment) x 100%

- Time Frame: Consider both short-term and long-term ROI to evaluate potential growth.

- Leverage Impact: Account for the effects of financing on ROI, including interest rates and loan terms.

5. Legal and Zoning Considerations

Understanding legal and zoning regulations is crucial to avoid potential issues and ensure the property can be used as intended.

Key Considerations:

- Zoning Laws: Verify the property's zoning designation and permissible uses.

- Permits and Approvals: Ensure all necessary permits and approvals are in place for any modifications or intended uses.

- Legal Encumbrances: Check for liens,

- easements, or other legal encumbrances that could affect the property's use or value.

- Compliance: Ensure the property complies with local building codes and regulations.

6. Potential for Appreciation

Evaluating a property's potential for appreciation involves analyzing factors that could increase its value over time. This includes both intrinsic factors related to the property itself and extrinsic factors related to the surrounding area.

Key Considerations:

- Neighborhood Growth: Areas with increasing development, improving infrastructure, and rising demand are likely to see property values appreciate.

- Property Improvements: Upgrading or renovating the property can enhance its value.

- Market Conditions: Favorable market conditions, such as low-interest rates and strong economic growth, can drive appreciation.

- Historical Trends: Review historical appreciation rates in the area to gauge future potential.

7. Rental Yield

Rental yield measures the annual rental income as a percentage of the property's purchase price. It helps investors compare the income potential of different properties.

Key Considerations:

- Formula: Rental Yield = (Annual Rental Income / Purchase Price) x 100%

- Gross vs. Net Yield: Gross yield considers only the rental income, while net yield accounts for expenses.

- Comparative Analysis: Compare rental yields of similar properties to identify attractive investment opportunities.

8. Tenant Quality

The quality of tenants significantly impacts the stability and profitability of a rental property. High-quality tenants are more likely to pay rent on time, take care of the property, and stay for longer periods.

Key Considerations:

- Screening Process: Implement a thorough screening process to assess tenant reliability and financial stability.

- Rental History: Review potential tenants' rental history for any red flags.

- Employment Verification: Verify employment and income to ensure tenants can afford the rent.

- References: Check references from previous landlords and employers.

9. Exit Strategy

Having a clear exit strategy is essential for managing risk and maximizing returns. An exit strategy outlines how and when you plan to sell the property or transition it to another use.

Key Considerations:

- Market Timing: Monitor market conditions to identify the optimal time to sell.

- Value-Add Opportunities: Identify ways to increase the property's value before selling.

- Alternative Uses: Consider other potential uses for the property, such as redevelopment or conversion to a different type of rental.

- Tax Implications: Understand the tax implications of selling the property and plan accordingly.

10. Professional Assistance

Working with professionals can streamline the property evaluation process and provide valuable insights.

Key Considerations:

- Real Estate Agents: Leverage their market knowledge and negotiation skills.

- Property Inspectors: Conduct thorough inspections to identify potential issues.

- Appraisers: Obtain professional appraisals to determine the property's market value.

- Financial Advisors: Consult with advisors to analyze the investment's financial performance and plan for tax implications.

Investing in real estate requires a comprehensive approach to property search and evaluation. Utilizing both online and offline strategies ensures a wide range of options, while thorough evaluation based on key criteria and metrics helps in making informed decisions. By considering factors such as location, property condition, market trends, financial metrics, and potential for appreciation, investors can identify properties that align with their investment goals and maximize their returns.

Making Offers: Negotiation Techniques

The process of making an offer on a property is a critical phase in real estate transactions. Effective negotiation techniques can make a significant difference in securing a favorable deal. Here, we will explore various strategies to enhance your negotiation

skills and improve the chances of a successful offer.
Understanding the Market

Before making an offer, it is essential to understand the current market conditions. The real estate market can be classified into three main types:

- Buyer's Market: In a buyer's market, there are more properties available than buyers. This oversupply gives buyers an advantage, as sellers may be more willing to negotiate on price and terms.

- Seller's Market: In a seller's market, the demand for properties exceeds the supply. This situation gives sellers the upper hand, often resulting in higher prices and less room for negotiation.

- Balanced Market: A balanced market exists when the supply of properties is roughly equal to the demand. Negotiation in such a market may be more balanced, with both buyers and sellers having equal leverage.

To gauge the market, analyze factors such as inventory levels, average days on market, and recent sale prices of comparable properties (comps).
Preparing Your Offer

A well-prepared offer includes several key components:

- Price: The price you are willing to pay is the most critical element of your offer. Base your offer price on a thorough analysis of comparable properties, market conditions, and the property's condition.

- Contingencies: Contingencies are conditions that must be met for the sale to proceed. Common contingencies include financing, inspection, and appraisal contingencies. These protect you from unforeseen issues and allow you to withdraw your offer if necessary.

- Earnest Money Deposit: This is a deposit made to show your serious intent to purchase the property. It is typically held in escrow and applied to the purchase price at closing. A higher earnest money deposit can make your offer more attractive to sellers.

- Closing Date: Specify a closing date that aligns with your timeline and the seller's preferences. Flexibility in closing dates can be a valuable negotiating tool.

- Additional Terms: Include any other terms or requests, such as asking the seller to cover certain closing costs or include specific appliances in the sale.

Strategies for Effective Negotiation

Negotiation is both an art and a science. Here are some strategies to enhance your negotiation skills:

- Do Your Homework: Research the property's history, the seller's situation, and the local market. Understanding the seller's motivations (e.g., a quick sale, relocating, financial constraints) can provide valuable insights for negotiation.

- Build Rapport: Establish a positive relationship with the seller or their agent. Building trust and demonstrating respect can create a more cooperative negotiation environment.

- Be Confident but Realistic: Confidence is essential in negotiation, but so is realism. Make sure your offer is competitive and justifiable based on market data.

- Start with a Strong Offer: A strong initial offer can set a positive tone for negotiations. However, avoid starting too high, as this leaves little room for further negotiation.

- Be Prepared to Compromise: Flexibility is crucial in negotiation. Identify your must-haves and nice-to-haves, and be willing to make concessions on less critical issues.

- Use Deadlines: Setting deadlines for responses can create a sense of urgency and prompt the other party to act more quickly.

- Leverage Multiple Offers: If you are interested in multiple properties, let the sellers know you are considering other options. This can create a sense of competition and urgency.

- Stay Calm and Professional: Emotions can run

high during negotiations, but maintaining composure and professionalism is key. Avoid aggressive tactics that can alienate the other party.

Handling Counteroffers

Receiving a counteroffer is common in real estate negotiations. When you receive a counteroffer:

- Review Carefully: Assess the counteroffer thoroughly, considering changes in price, contingencies, and terms.

- Respond Promptly: Delays can cause negotiations to stall or fall apart. Respond to counteroffers in a timely manner.

- Negotiate Further if Necessary: If the counteroffer is not satisfactory, propose further adjustments. Continue negotiating until both parties reach an agreement or decide to walk away.

- Know When to Walk Away: Sometimes, despite best efforts, a mutually acceptable agreement cannot be reached. Know your limits and be prepared to walk away if the terms are not favorable.

Due Diligence: Inspections and Appraisals

Due diligence is a critical phase in the property purchasing process. It involves conducting thorough inspections and appraisals to ensure the property is in good condition and valued accurately. This section will delve into the importance of due diligence, the types of inspections and appraisals, and how to navigate this phase effectively.

Importance of Due Diligence

Due diligence helps protect your investment by uncovering potential issues with the property that may not be apparent at first glance. It ensures that you are fully informed about the property's condition and value before finalizing the purchase. Skipping due diligence can lead to costly surprises and regrets later on.

Types of Inspections

Several types of inspections can be conducted during the due diligence period. Each serves a specific purpose in evaluating different aspects of the property:

- General Home Inspection: A general home inspection is a comprehensive assessment of the property's overall condition. A licensed home inspector will examine the structural components, electrical systems, plumbing, heating and cooling systems, roof, foundation, and more.

- Pest Inspection: Pest inspections focus on identifying infestations of termites, rodents, and other pests. These inspections are crucial, as pest damage can compromise the structural integrity of the property.

- Mold Inspection: Mold inspections check for the presence of mold, which can pose health risks and indicate underlying moisture problems.

- Radon Inspection: Radon inspections measure radon levels in the property. Radon is a radioactive gas that can cause lung cancer, making this inspection particularly important in certain regions.

- Lead Paint Inspection: For older properties, lead paint inspections determine the presence of lead-based paint, which can be hazardous, especially for children.

- Sewer and Septic Inspection: These inspections evaluate the condition of the property's sewer lines and septic system to ensure proper functioning and avoid potential issues.

- Chimney Inspection: Chimney inspections check for blockages, structural integrity, and the condition of the flue and liner.

- Pool Inspection: If the property has a pool, a pool inspection assesses the condition of the pool, its equipment, and safety features.

Choosing a Home Inspector

Selecting a qualified and experienced home inspector is crucial to ensuring a thorough evaluation of the property. Consider the following when choosing a home inspector:

- Certifications and Licenses: Ensure the inspector is licensed and certified by reputable organizations, such as the American Society of Home Inspectors (ASHI) or the International Association of Certified Home Inspectors (InterNACHI).

- Experience: Look for an inspector with extensive experience in the field. Experienced inspectors are more likely to identify potential issues accurately.

- References: Ask for references from previous clients to gauge the inspector's reliability and thoroughness.

- Sample Reports: Request a sample inspection report to see the level of detail provided. A good report should be comprehensive and include photos and explanations of any issues found.

- Insurance: Verify that the inspector carries professional liability insurance, also known as errors and omissions (E&O) insurance, to cover any potential mistakes.

Conducting the Inspection

During the inspection, it is advisable to be present to ask questions and gain a better understanding of the property's condition. The inspector will provide a detailed report outlining any issues discovered. Key areas to focus on include:

- Structural Components: Check for cracks, sagging, or other signs of structural damage in the foundation, walls, and roof.

- Roof and Attic: Inspect for leaks, damaged shingles, and proper ventilation in the attic.

- Electrical Systems: Ensure the electrical panel, wiring, and outlets are up to code and functioning safely.

- Plumbing: Look for leaks, water pressure issues, and the condition of pipes and fixtures.

- HVAC Systems: Assess the heating, ventilation, and air conditioning systems for age, efficiency, and any maintenance needs.

- Windows and Doors: Check for proper operation, seals, and any signs of damage or drafts.

- Basement and Crawl Spaces: Look for moisture, mold, or pest issues in these areas.

Reviewing the Inspection Report

Once you receive the inspection report, review it carefully to understand the severity and implications of any issues found. Consider the following steps:

- Prioritize Repairs: Identify which issues are critical and require immediate attention versus those that are minor and can be addressed later.

- Get Estimates: For significant repairs, obtain estimates from contractors to understand the potential costs involved.

- Negotiate with the Seller: Use the inspection report to negotiate with the seller. You may request repairs, a price reduction, or credits at closing to cover the cost of necessary repairs.

- Revisit Your Offer: Based on the inspection findings, you may need to revisit your offer and make adjustments accordingly. If the issues are too severe, you might decide to walk away from the deal.

Appraisals

An appraisal is an independent assessment of the property's market value conducted by a licensed appraiser. Lenders typically require an appraisal to ensure the property's value supports the loan amount. The appraisal process involves several steps:

- Order the Appraisal: The lender will order the appraisal, but you may choose to hire your appraiser for an independent evaluation.

- Property Inspection: The appraiser visits the property to conduct a visual inspection, taking note of its condition, features, and any improvements or upgrades.

- Comparative Market Analysis: The appraiser analyzes comparable properties (comps) that have recently sold in the area to determine the property's value. Factors considered include size, location, condition, and amenities.

- Appraisal Report: The appraiser compiles the findings into a detailed report, which includes the appraised value, a description of the property, and information about the comps used.

Reviewing the Appraisal Report

The appraisal report is a critical document that influences the loan approval process. Key sections to review include:

- Appraised Value: Compare the appraised value to your offer price. If the appraisal is lower than expected, you may need to renegotiate with the seller or increase your down payment to bridge the gap.

- Comparable Sales: Review the comps used by the appraiser. Ensure they are recent and similar to the property you are purchasing.

- Condition and Comments: Take note of any comments the appraiser made about the property's condition or any factors that influenced the valuation.

Addressing Low Appraisals

If the appraisal comes in lower than the purchase price, several options are available:

- Renegotiate the Price: Use the appraisal as leverage to negotiate a lower purchase price with the seller.

- Challenge the Appraisal: If you believe the appraisal is inaccurate, you can request a review or a second appraisal. Provide additional comps or information to support your case.

- Increase the Down Payment: If renegotiating the price is not an option, you may need to increase your down payment to meet the lender's loan-to-value (LTV) requirements.

- Seek Alternative Financing: Explore other financing options or lenders who may be willing to work with the existing appraisal.

Finalizing Due Diligence

Completing due diligence involves several final steps to ensure a smooth transaction:

- Review All Reports: Carefully review all inspection and appraisal reports, addressing any concerns or discrepancies.

- Finalize Negotiations: Based on the findings, finalize any negotiations with the seller regarding repairs, price adjustments, or credits.

- Confirm Financing: Ensure your financing is in place, and the lender has all necessary documentation, including the appraisal report.

- Prepare for Closing: Work with your real estate agent, attorney, and lender to prepare for the closing process. This includes finalizing the purchase agreement, conducting a final walk-through, and reviewing closing documents.

- Schedule a Final Walk-Through: A final walk-through allows you to verify that any agreed-upon repairs have been completed and that the property is in the expected condition before closing.

Due diligence is a vital step in the real estate buying process. Thorough inspections and accurate appraisals help ensure you are making an informed investment and protect you from unforeseen issues. By understanding the importance of due diligence and following best practices for inspections and appraisals, you can navigate this phase confidently and secure a property that meets your needs and expectations.

Chapter 5:

Acquisitions and Closings

The acquisition process in real estate involves several critical steps from making an offer to ultimately taking ownership of a property. This process can be intricate, involving legal, financial, and procedural aspects that must be meticulously navigated to ensure a successful transaction. Here, we will explore the comprehensive journey of acquiring a property, highlighting key phases and considerations along the way.

1. The Acquisition Process: From Offer to Ownership
Making the Offer

1.1 Research and Preparation

Before making an offer on a property, thorough research and preparation are essential. This includes understanding the market, assessing the property's value, and determining your financial capabilities. Key steps in this phase include:

- Market Analysis: Evaluate current market conditions, recent sales of comparable properties, and local trends to gauge a fair offer price.

- Financial Readiness: Ensure your financing is in order, whether through pre-approval for a mortgage or having sufficient funds available if paying in cash.

- Property Evaluation: Review the property's details, including its condition, location, and potential for appreciation.

1.2 Crafting the Offer

Once you are ready to make an offer, several components need to be carefully crafted to present a strong and competitive proposal:

- Offer Price: Base your offer price on your market analysis and the property's condition. Consider leaving room for negotiation.

- Contingencies: Include contingencies to protect your interests, such as inspection, financing, and appraisal contingencies.

- Earnest Money Deposit: Offer a substantial earnest money deposit to demonstrate your serious intent to purchase the property.

- Terms and Conditions: Clearly outline the terms and conditions of the offer, including the proposed closing date and any requests for seller concessions.

1.3 Submitting the Offer

Your real estate agent will submit the offer to the seller or the seller's agent. This initiates the negotiation phase, where the seller may accept, reject, or counter your offer. Be prepared for back-and-forth discussions to reach mutually acceptable terms.

Negotiation and Contract

1.4 Negotiation Tactics

Effective negotiation is crucial to securing a favorable deal. Consider the following tactics:

- Be Flexible: Identify your non-negotiables but remain flexible on other terms to facilitate a compromise.

- Understand Seller's Motivations: Gain insights into the seller's motivations, such as a desire for a quick sale or specific closing date preferences, to tailor your negotiation approach.

- Maintain Professionalism: Keep negotiations professional and respectful, focusing on finding common ground.

1.5 Reaching an Agreement

Once both parties agree on the terms, the offer is formalized into a purchase agreement. This legally binding contract outlines all agreed-upon terms, including the price, contingencies, and timelines. Key elements of the purchase agreement include:

- Purchase Price: The agreed-upon price for the property.
- Contingencies: Conditions that must be met for the sale to proceed.
- Closing Date: The date by which the transaction must be completed.
- Property Inclusions: Items included in the sale, such as appliances or fixtures.
- Earnest Money Deposit: The amount and conditions for the earnest money deposit.

Due Diligence

1.6 Property Inspections

The due diligence phase involves conducting thorough inspections to identify any potential issues with the property. Common inspections include:

- General Home Inspection: A comprehensive evaluation of the property's overall condition.
- Specialized Inspections: Additional inspections for specific concerns, such as pest, mold, or radon inspections.

1.7 Reviewing Inspection Reports

After receiving the inspection reports, review them carefully to understand the property's condition and any necessary repairs. Based on the findings, you may:

- Negotiate Repairs: Request the seller to address specific issues or provide a credit for repairs.

- Adjust the Offer: If significant issues are discovered, you may renegotiate the price or terms.

- Proceed or Withdraw: Decide whether to move forward with the purchase or withdraw your offer based on the inspection results.

1.8 Appraisal

If you are financing the purchase, the lender will require an appraisal to determine the property's value. The appraisal ensures that the loan amount is appropriate relative to the property's worth. Key steps include:

- Order the Appraisal: The lender orders the appraisal, and a licensed appraiser evaluates the property.

- Review the Appraisal Report: Examine the appraised value and ensure it aligns with your offer price. If the appraisal is lower than expected, renegotiate with the seller or increase your down payment.

Finalizing Financing

1.9 Securing the Loan

Once the appraisal is complete and satisfactory, work with your lender to finalize the loan. This involves:

- Providing Documentation: Submit all required documentation, including income verification, tax returns, and bank statements.
- Loan Underwriting: The lender's underwriting team reviews your application and documentation to approve the loan.//
- Loan Approval: Once approved, the lender issues a loan commitment letter outlining the terms and conditions of the mortgage.

1.10 Reviewing Loan Documents

Carefully review all loan documents, including the loan estimate and closing disclosure, to understand the terms, interest rates, and closing costs. Ensure all details are accurate and consistent with your expectations.

Preparing for Closing

1.11 Title Search and Insurance

A title search is conducted to ensure the property's title is clear of any liens, encumbrances, or legal issues. Once the title is verified, obtain title insurance to protect against any future claims or disputes.

1.12 Final Walk-Through

Schedule a final walk-through of the property a few days before closing to ensure it is in the agreed-upon condition and any requested repairs have been completed.

1.13 Preparing Closing Documents

Work with your real estate agent, attorney, and lender to prepare all necessary closing documents. These include:

- Deed: The legal document transferring ownership of the property.

- Bill of Sale: A document listing any personal property included in the sale.

- Closing Disclosure: A detailed statement of all closing costs and financial transactions.

Closing the Deal

1.14 Attending the Closing

The closing is the final step in the acquisition process, where all parties sign the necessary documents to complete the transaction. Key participants at the closing typically include:

- Buyer: You, the purchaser of the property.

- Seller: The current owner of the property.

- Real Estate Agents: Representatives for both the buyer and the seller.

- Closing Agent or Attorney: A neutral third party who facilitates the closing process.

- Lender: The financial institution providing the mortgage.

1.15 Signing Documents

At the closing, you will sign various documents, including:

- Closing Disclosure: Confirming the accuracy of the financial details.

- Mortgage Note: A promise to repay the loan according to specified terms.

- Deed of Trust: Securing the mortgage by placing a lien on the property.

- Affidavits and Declarations: Verifying certain aspects of the transaction, such as your identity and intentions.

1.16 Transferring Funds

Funds are transferred to complete the purchase. This includes:

- Down Payment: Your contribution to the purchase price.

- Closing Costs: Fees associated with the transaction, such as title insurance, attorney fees, and lender charges.

- Loan Proceeds: The mortgage amount provided by the lender.

1.17 Receiving the Keys

Once all documents are signed and funds are transferred, the closing agent records the deed with the local government, officially transferring ownership to you. You then receive the keys to your new property.

Post-Closing Considerations

Recording and Filing

After the closing, the deed and mortgage documents are recorded with the local county recorder's office. This ensures public record of the transaction and your ownership.
Moving In

Plan and coordinate your move-in process, including:

- Scheduling Movers: Arrange professional movers or rent a moving truck.

- Setting Up Utilities: Transfer or establish utility services in your name.

- Address Change: Update your address with the

post office, banks, and other important institutions.

Property Management

If the property is an investment, establish a property management plan:

- Tenant Screening: If renting, implement a thorough tenant screening process.

- Maintenance: Set up regular maintenance schedules to keep the property in good condition.

- Financial Management: Keep detailed records of income and expenses for tax purposes and financial planning.

Review and Reflect

After acquiring the property, take time to review the entire acquisition process:

- Evaluate the Experience: Reflect on what went well and areas for improvement in future acquisitions.

- Update Your Strategy: Adjust your real estate investment strategy based on lessons learned and market changes.

- Celebrate Your Success: Acknowledge the achievement of acquiring a new property and its potential benefits to your portfolio.

The acquisition process in real estate, from making an offer to taking ownership, is a multifaceted journey that requires careful planning, negotiation, and execution. By understanding each phase and its key components, you can navigate the complexities of real estate transactions with confidence. Whether you are a first-time buyer or an experienced investor, following a structured approach ensures a successful acquisition and sets the foundation for future real estate endeavors.

Working with Agents and Brokers: Leveraging Professional Help

The Role of Agents and Brokers

Real estate agents and brokers play a crucial role in the property acquisition process. Their expertise, local market knowledge, and negotiation skills can significantly enhance your chances of finding and securing the right property at the best price. Here, we will delve into the various benefits of working with these professionals and how to effectively leverage their help.

Real Estate Agents vs. Brokers

It is important to distinguish between real estate agents and brokers, as their roles and responsibilities differ slightly:

- Real Estate Agents: Agents are licensed professionals who assist buyers and sellers in real estate transactions. They typically work under the supervision of a licensed broker.

- Real Estate Brokers: Brokers have additional education and experience beyond that of an agent. They can work independently and hire agents to work under them. Brokers are often involved in more complex transactions and have a deeper understanding of real estate laws and practices.

Benefits of Working with Real Estate Professionals

Market Knowledge and Expertise

Real estate agents and brokers possess extensive knowledge of the local market, including current trends, property values, and neighborhood insights. This expertise allows them to:

- Identify Opportunities: Agents and brokers can pinpoint properties that match your criteria, including those that may not be widely advertised.

- Provide Comparables: They can provide comparative market analyses (CMAs) to help you understand the fair market value of properties.

- Offer Market Insights: Agents and brokers can offer valuable insights into neighborhood amenities, school districts, and future development plans.

Access to Listings

One of the significant advantages of working with real estate professionals is their access to multiple listing services (MLS). MLS databases contain comprehensive property listings that are not always available to the general public. This access allows agents and brokers to:

- Find Off-Market Properties: Agents and brokers often have knowledge of properties that are not yet listed or are being sold privately.

- Set Up Alerts: They can set up automated alerts to notify you of new listings that meet your criteria.

- Schedule Viewings: Agents and brokers can arrange property viewings, often giving you early access before properties are widely advertised.

Negotiation Skills

Negotiating the purchase price and terms of a property is a critical aspect of the acquisition process. Real estate agents and brokers are skilled negotiators who can:

- Advocate for Your Interests: They represent your interests in negotiations with sellers and their agents.

- Utilize Market Data: Agents and brokers use

market data to justify your offer price and negotiate favorable terms.

- Handle Counteroffers: They can effectively manage counteroffers, ensuring that the negotiations progress smoothly and in your favor.

Streamlined Process

The process of buying a property involves numerous steps, from making an offer to closing the deal. Real estate agents and brokers can streamline this process by:

- Coordinating Tasks: They coordinate various tasks, such as scheduling inspections, appraisals, and closing appointments.

- Managing Paperwork: Agents and brokers handle the extensive paperwork involved in real estate transactions, ensuring all documents are accurate and complete.

- Facilitating Communication: They act as a liaison between you and other parties involved in the transaction, such as lenders, inspectors, and attorneys.

Finding the Right Agent or Broker

Choosing the right real estate professional is crucial to the success of your property acquisition. Consider the following factors when selecting an agent or broker: Experience and Track Record

- Years in Business: Look for agents or brokers with several years of experience in the local market.

- Transaction History: Review their transaction history to gauge their success in handling similar properties.

- Specializations: Some agents and brokers specialize in specific types of properties or neighborhoods. Choose one with expertise relevant to your needs.

Reputation and References

- Client Reviews: Read reviews and testimonials from previous clients to assess their satisfaction with the agent or broker's services.

- Professional Reputation: Check for any disciplinary actions or complaints with local real estate boards or professional associations.

- References: Ask for references from past clients and follow up to learn about their experiences.

Communication and Compatibility

- Communication Style: Choose an agent or broker who communicates clearly and promptly. They should be accessible and responsive to your inquiries.

- Compatibility: Ensure you feel comfortable

working with the agent or broker. A good rapport can enhance collaboration and make the process more enjoyable.

Fees and Commission

- Commission Structure: Understand the agent or broker's commission structure and any additional fees. Typically, the seller pays the commission, which is split between the buyer's and seller's agents.

- Value for Money: Consider the value provided by the agent or broker relative to their fees. A skilled professional can often save you money by negotiating a better deal.

Maximizing the Relationship with Your Agent or Broker

Clear Communication

Effective communication is key to a successful partnership with your real estate agent or broker. Clearly articulate your needs, preferences, and budget. Regularly update them on any changes to your criteria or financial situation.

Be Prepared

Provide your agent or broker with all necessary documentation and information promptly. This includes pre-approval letters, proof of funds, and identification documents. Being prepared ensures a smoother process and demonstrates your seriousness as a buyer.

Trust Their Expertise

Trust your agent or broker's expertise and judgment. While it's important to do your own research, rely on their knowledge and experience to guide you through the complexities of the transaction.

Stay Engaged

Stay actively involved in the process. Attend property viewings, ask questions, and provide feedback. Your engagement helps your agent or broker understand your preferences better and tailor their search accordingly.

Understanding Contracts: Key Clauses and Terms

Real estate contracts are complex legal documents that outline the terms and conditions of a property transaction. Understanding key clauses and terms in these contracts is essential to protect your interests and ensure a smooth transaction. This section will explore the critical components of real estate contracts and their significance.

Key Components of Real Estate Contracts

Purchase Price and Payment Terms

- Purchase Price: The agreed-upon amount that the buyer will pay for the property. This is the most critical term in the contract.

- Earnest Money Deposit: A deposit made by the buyer to demonstrate their serious intent to purchase. This amount is typically held in escrow and applied to the purchase price at closing.

- Payment Terms: Details on how the purchase price will be paid, including the amount of any down payment, financing arrangements, and the schedule of payments.

Contingencies

Contingencies are conditions that must be met for the contract to be legally binding. Common contingencies include:

- Inspection Contingency: Allows the buyer to have the property inspected by a professional and negotiate repairs or cancel the contract if significant issues are found.

- Financing Contingency: Protects the buyer if they are unable to secure financing. If the buyer cannot obtain a mortgage, they can withdraw from the contract without penalty.

- Appraisal Contingency: Ensures that the property appraises for at least the purchase price. If the appraisal is lower, the buyer can renegotiate or cancel the contract.

- Sale of Buyer's Property Contingency: Allows the buyer to withdraw from the contract if they are unable to sell their current home within a specified timeframe.

Property Description and Inclusions

- Property Description: A detailed description of the property, including its address, legal description, and any specific features or improvements.

- Inclusions and Exclusions: Specifies which items are included or excluded in the sale, such as appliances, fixtures, and furniture.

Closing and Possession Dates

- Closing Date: The date by which the transaction must be completed, and ownership transferred to the buyer. This date is critical for coordinating financing, inspections, and other pre-closing activities.

- Possession Date: The date when the buyer takes physical possession of the property. This may or may not coincide with the closing date.

Title and Survey

- Title Commitment: A document provided by a title company that outlines the current status of the property's title, including any liens, encumbrances, or title defects. The contract should specify the type of title the seller must convey, typically a clear and marketable title.

- Survey: A survey may be required to verify the property's boundaries and identify any encroachments or easements. The contract should specify who is responsible for obtaining and paying for the survey.

Default and Remedies

- Default: The contract should outline what constitutes a default by either party and the consequences of such a default. For example, failure to close the transaction by the specified date may be considered a default.

- Remedies: Specifies the remedies available to the non-defaulting party. Common remedies include the return of the earnest money deposit, specific performance (forcing the sale), or monetary damages.

Additional Terms and Conditions

- Disclosures: The contract should include any required disclosures, such as lead-based paint disclosures for older homes or seller property condition disclosures.

- Warranties: Any warranties provided by the seller, such as a home warranty or warranties on specific appliances or systems.

- Amendments: The process for amending the contract, including how changes must be documented and agreed upon by both parties.

Understanding Common Contract Terms

As-Is

When a property is sold "as-is," the seller is not required to make any repairs or improvements to the property. The buyer accepts the property in its current condition, including any defects. It is crucial for buyers to conduct thorough inspections and due diligence when purchasing an as-is property.

Closing Costs

Closing costs are the fees and expenses associated with finalizing the property transaction. These may include:

- Title Insurance: Protects the buyer and lender against any future claims to the property's title.

- Escrow Fees: Fees charged by the escrow company for handling the transaction and distributing funds.
- Recording Fees: Fees for recording the deed and other documents with the local government.

- Loan Fees: Charges related to obtaining a mortgage, such as origination fees, appraisal fees, and discount points.

Deed

The deed is the legal document that transfers ownership of the property from the seller to the buyer. There are several types of deeds, including:

- Warranty Deed: Provides the highest level of protection to the buyer, guaranteeing that the seller has clear title and the right to sell the property.

- Quitclaim Deed: Transfers whatever interest the seller has in the property without any warranties. Often used to clear up title issues or transfer property between family members.

- Special Warranty Deed: Provides some protection, but only guarantees the title against claims arising during the seller's ownership.

Escrow

Escrow is a neutral third-party service that holds funds and documents related to the transaction until all conditions of the contract are met. The escrow company ensures that funds are disbursed appropriately and that all legal requirements are satisfied before closing.

Fixtures

Fixtures are items that are permanently attached to the property, such as built-in appliances, lighting fixtures, and plumbing fixtures. The contract should specify which fixtures are included in the sale and which are excluded.

Prorations

Prorations are adjustments made at closing to account for expenses that are paid in advance or in arrears. Common prorations include:

- Property Taxes: Adjusted based on the closing date, so each party pays their share of the annual tax bill.

- Homeowner Association (HOA) Fees: Prorated based on the closing date, so the seller pays up to the closing date, and the buyer pays from the closing date forward.

- Utilities: Adjusted to ensure the seller pays for utilities up to the closing date, and the buyer pays thereafter.

Key Clauses to Watch For

Inspection Clause

The inspection clause outlines the buyer's right to inspect the property and the process for addressing any issues discovered during the inspection. Key elements include:

- Inspection Period: The timeframe within which the buyer must complete inspections and notify the seller of any issues.

- Repair Requests: The process for requesting

repairs or negotiating credits based on inspection findings.

- Right to Withdraw: The buyer's right to withdraw from the contract if significant issues are discovered.

Financing Clause

The financing clause protects the buyer if they are unable to secure financing. Key elements include:

- Loan Approval Deadline: The date by which the buyer must obtain loan approval.

- Financing Terms: Specific terms of the loan, such as the interest rate, loan type, and down payment.

- Failure to Obtain Financing: The buyer's right to withdraw from the contract without penalty if they are unable to secure financing by the specified deadline.

Appraisal Clause

The appraisal clause protects the buyer if the property appraises for less than the purchase price. Key elements include:

- Appraisal Contingency Period: The timeframe within which the appraisal must be completed.

- Appraisal Value: The process for addressing a low appraisal, such as renegotiating the price or providing additional funds.

- Right to Withdraw: The buyer's right to withdraw from the contract if the appraisal is significantly lower than the purchase price.

Title Clause

The title clause outlines the requirements for the seller to provide clear title to the property. Key elements include:

- Title Commitment: The seller must provide a title commitment showing clear title and any exceptions.

- Title Defects: The process for addressing any title defects discovered during the title search.

- Title Insurance: The requirement for the seller to provide title insurance to protect the buyer against future claims.

Default Clause

The default clause specifies what constitutes a default by either party and the consequences of such a default. Key elements include:

- Buyer Default: Conditions under which the buyer is considered in default, such as failing to close by the specified date.

- Seller Default: Conditions under which the seller is considered in default, such as failing to provide clear title.

- Remedies: The remedies available to the non-defaulting party, such as returning the earnest money deposit or seeking monetary damages.

Working with real estate agents and brokers can significantly enhance your property acquisition process, providing valuable market insights, access to listings, and skilled negotiation. Understanding the key components and terms of real estate contracts is essential to protect your interests and ensure a smooth transaction. By leveraging professional help and being well-informed about contractual clauses, you can navigate the complexities of real estate transactions with confidence and success.

The Closing Process: Steps and What to Expect

The closing process is the final stage in the acquisition of a property. It involves a series of steps and detailed procedures that culminate in the transfer of property ownership from the seller to the buyer. Understanding the intricacies of the closing process helps ensure a smooth transition and mitigates potential issues. Here, we will explore the various steps involved and what to expect during this critical phase.

1. Preparing for Closing

Review the Closing Disclosure

A few days before closing, you will receive the Closing Disclosure form from your lender. This document provides a detailed account of the loan terms, including the interest rate, monthly payments, and closing costs. It is essential to review this form carefully to ensure all the information is accurate and matches the terms agreed upon in your loan estimate.

Key Elements to Review:

- Loan Terms: Verify the loan amount, interest rate, and type of loan.

- Monthly Payments: Ensure the monthly payments, including principal, interest, taxes, and insurance (PITI), are correct.

- Closing Costs: Check the breakdown of closing costs, including lender fees, title insurance, and escrow charges.

- Cash to Close: Confirm the total amount of money you need to bring to the closing.

Conduct a Final Walk-Through

A final walk-through is typically scheduled within 24 hours before closing. This is your last opportunity to inspect the property and ensure it is in the agreed-upon condition. During the walk-through, verify that all requested repairs have been completed, no new damage has occurred, and any items included in the sale are present.

Checklist for Final Walk-Through:

- Repairs: Confirm all agreed-upon repairs have

been made.

- Appliances and Fixtures: Ensure all included appliances and fixtures are in place and functioning.

- No New Damage: Check for any new damage that may have occurred since the last inspection.

- Personal Belongings: Ensure the seller has removed all personal belongings.

2. Attending the Closing

Closing Location and Attendees

The closing typically takes place at a title company office, an attorney's office, or a lender's office. The attendees usually include the buyer, seller, real estate agents, closing agent or attorney, and sometimes a lender representative.

Key Attendees:

- Buyer: You, the purchaser.

- Seller: The current property owner.

- Real Estate Agents: Representatives for both the buyer and seller.

- Closing Agent/Attorney: A neutral party facilitating the closing process.

- Lender Representative: May be present to address any last-minute loan issues.

Signing Documents

At the closing, you will sign various legal documents necessary to complete the transaction. These documents include the Closing Disclosure, promissory note, deed of trust, and other affidavits. The closing agent will guide you through each document, explaining its purpose and ensuring all required signatures are obtained.

Key Documents to Sign:

- Closing Disclosure: Finalizes the loan terms and costs.

- Promissory Note: Your promise to repay the loan.

- Deed of Trust/Mortgage: Secures the loan with the property as collateral.

- Affidavits: Legal statements verifying certain aspects of the transaction.

Transfer of Funds

Funds are transferred through a process called escrow. The buyer provides the required funds, including the down payment and closing costs, which are held in escrow until all conditions of the sale are met. The closing agent then disburses these funds to the appropriate parties, including the seller, real estate agents, and any other service providers involved in the transaction.

Steps in Fund Transfer:

- Wire Transfer: Arrange for a wire transfer of the required funds to the escrow account.

- Verification: The closing agent verifies receipt of the funds.

- Disbursement: Funds are disbursed to the seller, agents, and other parties.

3. Recording and Finalizing the Transaction

Recording the Deed

Once all documents are signed and funds are transferred, the closing agent records the deed with the local county recorder's office. This official recording transfers ownership of the property from the seller to the buyer and makes the transaction part of the public record.

Key Actions:

- Prepare Deed: The deed is prepared and signed by the seller.

- Submit for Recording: The closing agent submits the deed to the county recorder's office.

- Official Recording: The deed is officially

recorded, finalizing the transfer of ownership.

Issuing Title Insurance

Title insurance protects the buyer and lender against any future claims to the property's title. Once the deed is recorded, the title company issues the title insurance policy. This policy ensures that the title is clear and that there are no undisclosed liens, encumbrances, or legal issues affecting the property.

Types of Title Insurance:

- Owner's Title Insurance: Protects the buyer's ownership rights.
- Lender's Title Insurance: Protects the lender's interest in the property.

4. Post-Closing Tasks: Immediate Actions After Purchase

Completing the purchase of a property marks the beginning of several important post-closing tasks. These tasks ensure a smooth transition into ownership and help maintain the property's value. Here, we will discuss the immediate actions you should take after purchasing a property.

1. Secure and Change the Locks

One of the first tasks after closing is to secure your new property by changing the locks. This step ensures that you are the only one with access to the property. Additionally, consider reprogramming any electronic security systems or garage door openers.

Steps to Secure the Property:

- Change Locks: Hire a locksmith to change all exterior locks.

- Reprogram Security Systems: Update codes and settings for security systems and garage door openers.

- Install New Locks: Consider installing new locks or smart lock systems for added security.

2. Transfer Utilities and Services

Transferring utilities and setting up essential services is crucial to ensure your property is fully functional. Contact utility providers to transfer services into your name and schedule any necessary installations.

Utilities and Services to Transfer:

- Electricity and Gas: Contact the utility companies to transfer or establish service.

- Water and Sewer: Arrange for water and sewer services to be transferred.

- Trash and Recycling: Set up trash and recycling collection services.

- Internet and Cable: Schedule installation or transfer of internet and cable services.

3. Update Your Address

Updating your address with various organizations and service providers ensures you receive important correspondence and bills. Notify the following entities of your new address:

Entities to Notify:

- Postal Service: Submit a change of address form with the postal service.

- Banks and Financial Institutions: Update your address for all bank accounts, credit cards, and investment accounts.

- Employer: Notify your employer of your new address for payroll and benefits purposes.

- Insurance Providers: Update your address with health, auto, and any other insurance providers.

- Government Agencies: Notify the DMV, IRS, and any other relevant government agencies.

4. Review and Store Important Documents

After closing, you will receive a packet of important documents, including the deed, closing disclosure, and title insurance policy. Review these documents to ensure accuracy and store them in a safe place for future reference.

Key Documents to Review and Store:

- Deed: Confirms your ownership of the property.

- Closing Disclosure: Details the final terms and costs of the transaction.

- Title Insurance Policy: Provides protection against title defects.

- Loan Documents: Includes the promissory note and deed of trust/mortgage.

5. Schedule Necessary Repairs and Maintenance

Inspect the property thoroughly and schedule any necessary repairs or maintenance tasks. Addressing these issues promptly helps maintain the property's condition and prevents minor problems from becoming major repairs.

Common Repairs and Maintenance:

- HVAC Systems: Service heating and cooling systems to ensure they are functioning properly.
- Plumbing: Address any leaks or plumbing issues.

- Roof and Gutters: Inspect the roof and gutters for damage or debris and make necessary repairs.

- Landscaping: Maintain the yard and address any landscaping needs.

6. Establish a Property Management Plan

If the property is an investment or rental property, establish a property management plan to ensure it is well-maintained and generates consistent rental income. Consider hiring a professional property management company or handling the tasks yourself.

Key Elements of a Property Management Plan:

- Tenant Screening: Implement a thorough tenant screening process to select reliable tenants.

- Rent Collection: Establish a system for collecting rent and handling late payments.

- Maintenance and Repairs: Schedule regular maintenance and promptly address repair requests.

- Record Keeping: Keep detailed records of income, expenses, and tenant communications.

7. Familiarize Yourself with the Neighborhood

Getting to know your new neighborhood helps you settle in and become part of the community. Explore local amenities, meet your neighbors, and learn about the area's resources.

Steps to Familiarize Yourself:

- Explore: Walk or drive around the neighborhood to discover local parks, shops, and restaurants.

- Meet Neighbors: Introduce yourself to your neighbors and participate in community events.

- Join Local Groups: Join neighborhood associations, clubs, or online forums to stay informed about local news and activities.

8. Review Homeowners Association (HOA) Rules

If your property is part of a homeowners association (HOA), review the HOA rules and regulations to ensure compliance. Familiarize yourself with any fees, restrictions, and community guidelines.

Key Points to Review:

- Rules and Regulations: Review restrictions on property modifications, landscaping, and noise levels.

- Community Amenities: Learn about any amenities available to residents, such as pools, fitness centers, or parks.

- Meeting Schedules: Note the schedule for HOA meetings and consider attending to stay informed and involved in community decisions.

9. Verify Property Tax Information

Property taxes are a significant ongoing expense for homeowners. Verify your property tax information to ensure you understand your tax obligations and payment schedule.

Steps to Verify Property Tax Information:

- Tax Bill: Review your property tax bill for accuracy.
- Payment Schedule: Note the due dates for property tax payments.

- Escrow Account: If you have an escrow account with your mortgage, verify that your lender is making the payments on your behalf.

- Tax Exemptions: Investigate any tax exemptions or reductions you may qualify for, such as homestead exemptions or senior discounts.

10. Set Up a Home Maintenance Schedule

Regular home maintenance is crucial to preserving the value and functionality of your property. Establish a maintenance schedule to keep track of routine tasks and seasonal projects.

Sample Home Maintenance Schedule:

Monthly:

- HVAC Filters: Check and replace HVAC filters.
- Plumbing: Inspect for leaks and check water pressure.
- Smoke Detectors: Test smoke and carbon monoxide detectors.

Seasonal:

Spring:

- Landscaping: Trim trees and shrubs, fertilize the lawn.
- Gutters: Clean and inspect gutters and downspouts.
- AC System: Service air conditioning system.

Summer:

- Pest Control: Schedule pest control treatments.
- Roof Inspection: Check for any damage or wear.
- Exterior: Power wash siding and check for any repairs.

Fall:

- Furnace: Service heating system.

- Fireplace: Clean and inspect the fireplace and chimney.

- Winterize: Prepare plumbing and exterior faucets for winter.

Winter:

- Insulation: Check and add insulation where needed.

- Snow Removal: Arrange for snow removal services if necessary.

- Interior: Inspect and repair interior caulking and seals.

11. Update Home Insurance Policy

Ensure that your home insurance policy is updated to reflect the new property and provides adequate coverage. This includes both the structure and your personal belongings.

Steps to Update Home Insurance:

- Policy Review: Review your current home insurance policy for coverage details.

- New Coverage: Update the policy to include the new property, ensuring adequate coverage for the home and contents.

- Additional Coverage: Consider additional coverage for specific risks, such as flood or earthquake insurance.

- Discounts: Inquire about any available discounts, such as for security systems or bundling with other insurance policies.

12. Plan for Future Improvements

Consider any future improvements or renovations you may want to undertake to enhance the property's value or livability. Planning ahead allows you to budget and schedule these projects effectively.

Steps to Plan Future Improvements:

- Identify Priorities: List potential improvements, such as kitchen remodels, bathroom upgrades, or landscaping projects.

- Budgeting: Estimate the costs and create a budget for each project.

- Timeline: Develop a timeline for when you plan to complete each improvement.

- Permits: Research any permits or approvals required for your planned projects.

13. Financial Planning and Record Keeping

Proper financial planning and record-keeping are

essential for managing your property effectively, especially if it is an investment property. Maintain accurate records of all expenses, income, and important documents.

Key Financial Planning and Record Keeping Tasks:

- Expense Tracking: Keep detailed records of all property-related expenses, including repairs, maintenance, and utilities.

- Rental Income: Track rental income and maintain records of all transactions with tenants.

- Tax Planning: Consult with a tax professional to understand the tax implications of your property ownership and to maximize deductions.

- Document Storage: Store all important documents, such as the deed, insurance policies, and inspection reports, in a secure and organized manner.

14. Establish Emergency Contacts

Having a list of emergency contacts is crucial for handling any unexpected situations that may arise with your property. This includes contacts for repair services, utilities, and local authorities.

Essential Emergency Contacts:

- Utilities: Contact information for your utility providers (electricity, gas, water, sewer).

- Repair Services: Trusted contractors for plumbing, electrical, HVAC, and general repairs.

- Property Manager: If you have a property manager, their contact information for emergencies.

- Local Authorities: Contact information for local police, fire department, and medical services.

- Insurance: Your insurance provider's emergency claims number.

15. Introduce Yourself to Neighbors

Building good relationships with your neighbors can enhance your experience in your new home and create a supportive community. Take the time to introduce yourself and establish connections.

Steps to Introduce Yourself to Neighbors:

- Personal Introduction: Knock on doors and introduce yourself in person.

- Neighborhood Events: Attend local events or gatherings to meet more people.

- Community Involvement: Volunteer for neighborhood committees or projects.

- Contact Information: Exchange contact information with neighbors for emergencies or mutual assistance.

16. Plan for Future Property Management

If you plan to use the property as a rental or investment, consider future property management strategies to ensure it remains a profitable and well-maintained asset.

Property Management Strategies:

- Professional Management: Research and hire a reputable property management company if you prefer a hands-off approach.

- Self-Management: If managing the property yourself, develop a plan for tenant screening, rent collection, and maintenance.

- Long-Term Planning: Set long-term goals for the property, including potential upgrades, rent increases, and market analysis.

The closing process and post-closing tasks are critical components of successful property acquisition and management. By understanding the steps involved in closing, such as reviewing the Closing Disclosure, conducting a final walk-through, and signing necessary documents, you can ensure a smooth transition into ownership. Post-closing tasks, such as securing the property, transferring utilities, updating your address, and establishing a maintenance schedule, help maintain the property's value and functionality. Whether you are a first-time homebuyer or a seasoned investor, following these guidelines will set the foundation for successful property ownership and management.

Chapter 6:

Renovations and Property Improvements

Renovations and Property Improvements

Renovations and property improvements are integral to maximizing the value and functionality of real estate investments. Whether you are upgrading a newly acquired property or maintaining an existing one, planning and executing renovations effectively can significantly enhance the property's appeal and profitability. This section will focus on the crucial aspects of planning renovations, including budgeting and scheduling.

Planning Renovations: Budgeting and Scheduling

1. Assessing the Scope of Renovations

Before diving into the specifics of budgeting and scheduling, it's essential to assess the scope of the renovations needed. This involves a thorough evaluation of the property to identify areas that require improvement and to prioritize tasks based on their impact and urgency.

Key Areas to Assess:

- Structural Integrity: Ensure the foundation, roof, and overall structure are sound.

- Electrical Systems: Check wiring, outlets, and circuit breakers for safety and efficiency.

- Plumbing: Inspect pipes, faucets, and water heaters for leaks and functionality.

- HVAC Systems: Evaluate heating, ventilation, and air conditioning systems for performance and maintenance needs.

- Interior and Exterior Finishes: Examine walls, floors, windows, doors, and exterior siding for damage or wear.

2. Setting Renovation Goals

Define clear goals for your renovation project to guide your planning process. These goals should align with your overall investment strategy and consider factors such as market demand, property type, and long-term value.

Common Renovation Goals:

- Increase Property Value: Focus on improvements that add significant value to the property, such as kitchen remodels, bathroom upgrades, and adding living space.

- Enhance Aesthetics: Update the property's appearance to make it more attractive to potential buyers or tenants.

- Improve Functionality: Address functional issues to make the property more livable and efficient.

- Compliance and Safety: Ensure the property meets local building codes and safety regulations.

3. Creating a Renovation Plan

A detailed renovation plan serves as a roadmap for your project, outlining the scope, timeline, and resources required. This plan should be comprehensive and flexible, allowing for adjustments as needed.

Steps to Create a Renovation Plan:

- List of Tasks: Break down the renovation into specific tasks, such as replacing flooring, painting walls, or installing new fixtures.

- Prioritize Tasks: Rank tasks based on their importance and impact on the overall project.
- Estimate Costs: Determine the estimated cost for each task, considering materials, labor, permits, and contingencies.

- Set a Timeline: Develop a timeline that outlines the start and end dates for each task, ensuring that the sequence of activities is logical and efficient.

4. Budgeting for Renovations

Effective budgeting is crucial to ensure your renovation project stays on track financially. A well-planned budget helps you allocate resources efficiently and avoid unexpected expenses. Components of a Renovation Budget:

- Materials: Estimate the cost of all materials needed, such as lumber, paint, fixtures, and appliances.

- Labor: Account for the cost of hiring contractors, laborers, and any specialized tradespeople.

- Permits and Fees: Include the cost of obtaining necessary permits and paying any associated fees.

- Contingency Fund: Set aside a contingency fund (typically 10-20% of the total budget) to cover unexpected expenses or changes in scope.

- Miscellaneous Costs: Factor in additional costs, such as waste disposal, transportation, and equipment rentals.

Tips for Effective Budgeting:

- Get Multiple Quotes: Obtain quotes from several contractors and suppliers to ensure you are getting competitive prices.

- Track Expenses: Monitor your expenses throughout the project to stay within budget and make adjustments as needed.

- Avoid Over-Improvement: Ensure that your improvements are in line with the property's value and the neighborhood's standards to avoid over-investing.

5. Scheduling Renovations

A well-structured schedule is essential for keeping your renovation project on track and ensuring timely completion. Effective scheduling helps coordinate tasks, manage labor, and minimize disruptions.

Steps to Develop a Renovation Schedule:

- Identify Milestones: Set key milestones for significant stages of the project, such as demolition, framing, plumbing, electrical work, and finishing.

- Sequence Tasks: Arrange tasks in a logical sequence to ensure that each phase is completed before the next begins. For example, finish structural work before starting interior finishes.

- Allocate Time: Estimate the time required for each task and allocate sufficient time for completion, including buffer periods for unexpected delays.

- Coordinate with Contractors: Communicate the schedule with your contractors and ensure they are available and committed to the timeline.

Tips for Effective Scheduling:

- Be Realistic: Set achievable deadlines based on the complexity of the tasks and the availability of resources.

- Monitor Progress: Regularly review progress against the schedule and make adjustments as necessary to address any delays or issues.

- Maintain Flexibility: Be prepared to adapt the schedule to accommodate unforeseen challenges or changes in scope.

6. Hiring Contractors and Tradespeople

Choosing the right contractors and tradespeople is critical to the success of your renovation project. Quality workmanship and reliability are essential for ensuring that the project is completed on time and within budget.

Steps to Hire Contractors:

- Research and Referrals: Ask for referrals from friends, family, or real estate professionals and research potential contractors online.

- Check Credentials: Verify that contractors are licensed, insured, and bonded. Check their reputation and reviews from previous clients.

- Request Quotes: Obtain detailed quotes from multiple contractors, including a breakdown of costs for materials, labor, and any additional fees.

- Interview Candidates: Conduct interviews to assess their experience, communication skills, and willingness to work within your budget and timeline.

- Review Contracts: Carefully review the contract terms, including payment schedules, warranties, and scope of work, before signing.

7. Managing the Renovation Process

Effective project management is essential to ensure that your renovation project runs smoothly and stays on track. This involves regular communication, monitoring progress, and addressing issues promptly.

Key Aspects of Project Management:

- Communication: Maintain open and regular communication with your contractors, tradespeople, and any other stakeholders. Hold regular meetings to discuss progress, address concerns, and make decisions.

- Progress Monitoring: Regularly inspect the work to ensure it meets your standards and aligns with the renovation plan. Keep track of milestones and deadlines to ensure the project stays on schedule.

- Issue Resolution: Address any issues or obstacles promptly to avoid delays. This may involve making decisions on changes in scope, resolving conflicts, or managing unforeseen challenges.

- Documentation: Keep detailed records of all communications, agreements, expenses, and changes to the project. This documentation is essential for accountability and future reference.

8. Quality Control and Final Inspections

Ensuring quality control throughout the renovation process is crucial for achieving a high standard of workmanship and preventing future issues. Conducting final inspections helps verify that the work is completed to your satisfaction and meets all necessary standards.

Quality Control Measures:

- Regular Inspections: Conduct regular inspections at key stages of the project to assess the quality of work and address any deficiencies.

- Standards and Specifications: Clearly communicate your standards and specifications to contractors and ensure they are followed.

- Feedback and Corrections: Provide feedback to contractors and request corrections if the work does not meet your expectations.

Final Inspections:

- Punch List: Create a punch list of any remaining tasks, touch-ups, or corrections needed before finalizing the project.

- Professional Inspections: Consider hiring a professional inspector to verify that all work meets building codes and safety standards.

- Final Walk-Through: Conduct a final walk-through with your contractor to review the completed work and ensure all items on the punch list are addressed.

9. Completing the Renovation and Finalizing Payments

Once the renovation project is complete, it's important to finalize all outstanding payments and ensure all necessary documentation is in order. This marks the official conclusion of the renovation process.

Steps to Complete the Renovation:

- Review and Approval: Conduct a thorough review of the completed work and ensure all tasks are finished to your satisfaction.

- Final Payments: Make any final payments to

contractors and suppliers as per the agreed-upon terms. Ensure all receipts and invoices are collected and recorded.

- Release of Liens: Obtain a release of liens from contractors to ensure there are no claims against the property for unpaid work.

- Warranties and Guarantees: Ensure you receive all warranties and guarantees for materials, workmanship, and installed systems or appliances.

10. Post-Renovation Tasks

After completing the renovation, there are several important tasks to address to ensure the property is ready for its intended use, whether for sale, rental, or personal occupancy.

Post-Renovation Tasks:

- Cleaning and Staging: Thoroughly clean the property and stage it if you plan to sell or rent it. Staging enhances the property's appeal to potential buyers or tenants.

- Marketing: Develop a marketing strategy to promote the property. This may include listing it on real estate platforms, hosting open houses, and utilizing social media.

- Tenant Screening: If renting the property, implement a thorough tenant screening process to select reliable and responsible tenants.

- Maintenance Plan: Establish a maintenance plan to ensure the property remains in good condition. Schedule regular inspections and address any maintenance needs promptly.

Planning and executing renovations effectively is crucial to enhancing the value, functionality, and appeal of your property. By thoroughly assessing the scope of renovations, setting clear goals, creating a detailed renovation plan, and budgeting accurately, you can ensure your project stays on track financially and logistically. Effective scheduling, hiring reputable contractors, and managing the renovation process with attention to quality control and final inspections are essential to achieving successful outcomes. Finally, addressing post-renovation tasks ensures the property is ready for its intended use and maintains its value over time. By following these guidelines, you can navigate the complexities of renovations and property improvements with confidence and success.

Renovations and Property Improvements

Renovations are a pivotal aspect of real estate investment, offering the potential to significantly increase a property's value and appeal. However, deciding whether to undertake renovations yourself (DIY) or hire professionals can be a challenging decision. Additionally, focusing on key renovations that provide the highest return on investment (ROI) is crucial for maximizing profits. This section will explore the pros and cons of DIY versus hiring professionals and identify the renovations that add the most value to your property.

DIY vs. Hiring Professionals: Pros and Cons

When planning a renovation, one of the primary decisions is whether to do it yourself or hire professionals. Both approaches have their advantages and disadvantages, depending on the scope of the project, your skills, and the desired outcomes.

Pros and Cons of DIY

Pros

- Cost Savings
    - Lower Labor Costs: DIY projects eliminate labor costs, which can constitute a significant portion of the renovation budget.
    - Control Over Budget: Direct control over material choices and project scope can help manage expenses.

- Personal Satisfaction
    - Sense of Accomplishment: Completing a project yourself can be incredibly rewarding and satisfying.
    - Customization: You can tailor the renovation to your exact preferences and specifications.

- Flexibility

    - Flexible Schedule: Work on your own timeline without needing to coordinate with contractors.

    - Immediate Changes: Ability to make on-the-spot changes without waiting for contractor approval.

Cons

- Time-Consuming

    - Longer Project Duration: DIY projects often take longer to complete, especially if you have other commitments.

    - Learning Curve: Time spent learning new skills and troubleshooting problems can delay progress.

- Quality Concerns

    - Professional Finish: Achieving a professional-quality finish may be challenging without experience.

    - Mistakes: Errors can lead to additional costs for repairs or replacements.

- Limited Expertise

    - Specialized Skills: Certain tasks, such as electrical work or plumbing, require specialized knowledge and certifications.

- Regulatory Compliance: Ensuring the project complies with local building codes and regulations can be complex.

Pros and Cons of Hiring Professionals

Pros

- Expertise and Experience

    - Skilled Workmanship: Professionals bring expertise and experience, ensuring high-quality results.

    - Specialized Knowledge: Access to specialized skills for complex tasks, such as structural modifications and system installations.

- Time Efficiency

    - Faster Completion: Professionals can complete projects more quickly due to their experience and resources.

    - Project Management: Contractors manage the project, coordinating schedules, materials, and labor.

- Quality Assurance

    - Professional Standards: High standards of workmanship and adherence to best practices.

- Warranty and Insurance: Many contractors offer warranties on their work and carry insurance to cover any damages.

Cons

- Higher Costs

    - Labor Expenses: Hiring professionals increases costs due to labor fees.

    - Markup on Materials: Contractors may charge a markup on materials, raising overall expenses.

- Less Control

    - Limited Customization: You may have less control over the specifics of the project compared to DIY.

    - Communication Challenges: Miscommunications with contractors can lead to misunderstandings and errors.

- Dependency on Contractor's Schedule

    - Scheduling Delays: Project timelines are dependent on the contractor's availability and schedule.

- Potential for Overruns: Projects may experience delays due to unforeseen issues or contractor availability.

Key Considerations for Choosing Between DIY and Professionals

When deciding between DIY and hiring professionals, consider the following factors:

- Project Scope and Complexity

  - Small-Scale Projects: DIY may be suitable for small, manageable projects, such as painting or minor repairs.

  - Large-Scale Renovations: Hiring professionals is often necessary for extensive renovations requiring specialized skills.

- Budget Constraints

  - Limited Budget: DIY can help save money, but be mindful of potential hidden costs from mistakes.

  - Adequate Budget: Hiring professionals may be more cost-effective in the long run for complex projects.

- Time Availability

  - Flexible Schedule: If you have ample free time, DIY projects can be a rewarding endeavor.

- o Time Constraints: Hiring professionals is advisable if you have limited time or need the project completed quickly.

- Skill Level

    - o Experienced DIYer: If you have relevant skills and experience, DIY can be a viable option.

    - o Novice: For those with limited experience, hiring professionals ensures better results and safety.

Key Renovations for ROI: What Adds Value

Maximizing return on investment (ROI) is a primary goal for real estate investors. Certain renovations offer higher ROI by significantly enhancing the property's value and appeal. Identifying and prioritizing these key renovations is essential for maximizing profits.

High-ROI Renovations

1. Kitchen Remodel

A well-executed kitchen remodel can significantly increase a property's value. The kitchen is often considered the heart of the home, and modern, functional kitchens attract buyers and tenants alike.

Key Upgrades:

- Cabinets: Update or refinish cabinets for a fresh look.

- Countertops: Install durable and attractive countertops, such as granite or quartz.

- Appliances: Upgrade to energy-efficient, stainless steel appliances.

- Lighting: Enhance lighting with modern fixtures and under-cabinet lighting.

- Backsplash: Add a stylish backsplash for a touch of elegance.

ROI Potential: A minor kitchen remodel can recoup approximately 75-80% of its cost, while a major remodel can recoup about 60-70%.

2. Bathroom Remodel

Bathroom renovations are another high-ROI project. Updated bathrooms with modern amenities are highly appealing to buyers and renters.

Key Upgrades:

- Vanity: Replace or update the vanity with a contemporary design.

- Fixtures: Install new faucets, showerheads, and lighting fixtures.

- Tiles: Update flooring and shower tiles with durable, attractive options.

- Storage: Add built-in storage solutions for added convenience.

- Ventilation: Ensure proper ventilation to prevent moisture issues.

ROI Potential: A mid-range bathroom remodel can recoup about 65-70% of its cost, while an upscale remodel can recoup around 60%.

3. Curb Appeal Enhancements

First impressions matter, and improving curb appeal can significantly increase a property's perceived value. Simple exterior upgrades can make a big difference.

Key Upgrades:

- Landscaping: Maintain a well-manicured lawn, add plants, and install edging.

- Front Door: Replace or paint the front door to create an inviting entrance.

- Siding: Clean or replace siding to enhance the exterior appearance.

- Lighting: Install outdoor lighting to improve safety and aesthetics.

- Driveway and Walkways: Repair or resurface driveways and walkways.

ROI Potential: Curb appeal enhancements can recoup about 75-100% of their cost, depending on the extent of the improvements.

4. Energy-Efficient Upgrades

Energy-efficient upgrades reduce utility costs and appeal to environmentally conscious buyers and renters. These upgrades also often qualify for tax incentives and rebates.

Key Upgrades:

- Windows: Install energy-efficient windows to improve insulation.

- Insulation: Add or upgrade insulation in the attic, walls, and floors.

- HVAC Systems: Replace old HVAC systems with energy-efficient models.

- Water Heaters: Install tankless water heaters for on-demand hot water.

- Solar Panels: Consider installing solar panels to reduce energy costs.

ROI Potential: Energy-efficient upgrades can recoup about 60-80% of their cost, with potential for additional savings through energy cost reductions.

5. Adding Living Space

Increasing the usable living space in a property can significantly boost its value. This can be achieved through various means, such as finishing a basement or attic, adding a room, or constructing an accessory dwelling unit (ADU).

Key Upgrades:

- Basement: Finish the basement to create additional living or recreational space.
- Attic: Convert the attic into a bedroom or office.
- Room Addition: Add a new room, such as a family room or bedroom, to expand the living area.
- ADU: Construct an ADU for rental income or guest accommodation.

ROI Potential: Adding living space can recoup about 50-75% of its cost, depending on the type of addition and market conditions.

6. Outdoor Living Spaces

Outdoor living spaces are increasingly popular and can add significant value to a property. Creating functional and attractive outdoor areas enhances the overall appeal.

Key Upgrades:

- Deck or Patio: Build or update a deck or patio for outdoor entertaining.

- Outdoor Kitchen: Install an outdoor kitchen with a grill, sink, and countertop.

- Fire Pit: Add a fire pit or outdoor fireplace for year-round enjoyment.

- Pergola: Construct a pergola for shade and aesthetic appeal.

- Landscaping: Integrate landscaping elements to create a cohesive outdoor environment.

ROI Potential: Outdoor living space improvements can recoup about 60-75% of their cost.

7. Flooring Upgrades

Replacing outdated or worn flooring with modern, durable options can significantly enhance a property's appeal and value.

Key Upgrades:

- Hardwood Floors: Install or refinish hardwood floors for a timeless look.

- Tile: Use tile in high-traffic areas such as kitchens and bathrooms.

- Carpet: Replace old carpet with new, high-quality carpeting in bedrooms.

- Luxury Vinyl Plank (LVP): Install LVP flooring for a cost-effective, attractive option.

ROI Potential: Flooring upgrades can recoup about 70-80% of their cost, depending on the material and quality.

Factors Influencing ROI

Several factors influence the ROI of renovations. Understanding these factors can help you make informed decisions about which projects to undertake.

Market Conditions

The real estate market significantly impacts the ROI of renovations. In a seller's market, where demand is high, renovations may yield a higher ROI. Conversely, in a buyer's market, the ROI may be lower due to increased competition.

Property Location

Location plays a crucial role in determining the ROI of renovations. Properties in desirable neighborhoods or growing markets are more likely to see a higher return on improvements.

Quality of Work

The quality of workmanship and materials used in renovations directly affects the ROI. High-quality work and materials tend to yield a better return and reduce the likelihood of future repairs.

Property Type

Different property types may benefit from different renovations. For example, luxury properties may see higher ROI from upscale renovations, while mid-range properties may benefit more from cost-effective improvements.

Buyer Preferences

Understanding the preferences of potential buyers or renters in your target market is essential. Tailoring renovations to meet these preferences can enhance the property's appeal and increase ROI.

Deciding between DIY and hiring professionals for renovations involves weighing the pros and cons of each approach. DIY projects can save money and provide personal satisfaction, but they may require more time and carry risks of lower quality. Hiring professionals offers expertise and efficiency but comes at a higher cost. Ultimately, the decision depends on the project's scope, your skills, budget, and time availability.

Focusing on key renovations that provide the highest ROI is crucial for maximizing property value. Kitchen and bathroom remodels, curb appeal enhancements, energy-efficient upgrades, adding living space, outdoor living areas, and flooring upgrades are among the top renovations that can significantly boost a property's value. By considering market conditions, property location, quality of work, property type, and buyer preferences, you can make informed decisions about which renovations to undertake. These strategies will help you enhance your property's appeal, increase its value, and achieve a higher return on investment.

Managing Renovations: Timelines and Quality Control

Effective management of renovation projects is crucial to ensure they are completed on time, within budget, and to a high standard of quality. This involves meticulous planning, coordination, and monitoring of various aspects of the project. In this section, we will discuss strategies for managing renovation timelines and maintaining quality control throughout the process.

1. Developing a Detailed Renovation Plan

A well-structured renovation plan is the foundation of successful project management. This plan should outline all tasks, assign responsibilities, and establish a timeline for completion.

Components of a Renovation Plan:

- Scope of Work: Clearly define the scope of the renovation, detailing all tasks and objectives.

- Task Breakdown: Break down the project into manageable tasks and sub-tasks.

- Timeline: Create a timeline that includes start and end dates for each task.

- Budget: Outline the budget for each task and the overall project.

- Resource Allocation: Assign responsibilities to team members or contractors.

2. Establishing a Timeline

Creating a realistic timeline is essential for managing renovations effectively. The timeline should account for the sequence of tasks, dependencies, and potential delays.

Steps to Establish a Timeline:

- Identify Tasks: List all tasks required to complete the renovation.

- Sequence Tasks: Arrange tasks in a logical sequence, considering dependencies (e.g., plumbing work before drywall installation).

- Estimate Durations: Estimate the time required for each task.

- Set Milestones: Establish key milestones to track progress and ensure timely completion.

- Include Buffer Time: Allocate buffer time to account for unforeseen delays or issues.

Tools for Timeline Management:

- Gantt Charts: Visualize the project timeline and

task dependencies using Gantt charts.

- Project Management Software: Utilize software like Microsoft Project, Trello, or Asana to manage timelines and tasks.

- Calendars: Maintain a project calendar to track important dates and deadlines.

3. Coordinating with Contractors and Suppliers

Effective coordination with contractors and suppliers is crucial for maintaining the project timeline and ensuring quality work.

Communication Strategies:

- Regular Meetings: Schedule regular meetings with contractors to discuss progress, address issues, and adjust plans as needed.

- Clear Instructions: Provide clear and detailed instructions to contractors and suppliers.

- Contact List: Maintain a contact list of all contractors, suppliers, and team members for easy communication.

Contract Management:

- Written Contracts: Ensure all agreements with contractors and suppliers are documented in written contracts.

- Scope of Work: Clearly define the scope of work, deliverables, and deadlines in the contract.

- Payment Terms: Outline payment terms and schedules, tying payments to specific milestones or deliverables.

4. Monitoring Progress and Quality Control

Regular monitoring of progress and quality control is essential to ensure the renovation meets the required standards and stays on track.
Progress Monitoring:

- Site Visits: Conduct regular site visits to inspect work and monitor progress.

- Progress Reports: Request regular progress reports from contractors.

- Milestone Reviews: Review progress at key milestones to ensure tasks are completed on time.

Quality Control Measures:

- Standards and Specifications: Establish clear quality standards and specifications for materials and workmanship.

- Inspections: Schedule inspections at critical stages of the project to verify quality and compliance with standards.

- Feedback: Provide timely feedback to contractors and address any issues promptly.

5. Managing Changes and Issues

Renovation projects often encounter changes and issues that need to be managed effectively to avoid delays and cost overruns.

Change Management:

- Change Requests: Implement a formal process for managing change requests. Require written documentation for all changes.

- Impact Assessment: Assess the impact of changes on the timeline, budget, and scope before approval.

- Approval Process: Establish an approval process for changes, involving key stakeholders.

Issue Resolution:

- Issue Log: Maintain an issue log to track and manage problems as they arise.

- Root Cause Analysis: Conduct root cause analysis to identify and address the underlying causes of issues.

- Corrective Actions: Implement corrective actions promptly to minimize impact on the project.

6. Final Inspections and Handover

Upon completion of the renovation, conduct final inspections and ensure a smooth handover of the property.

Final Inspections:

- Punch List: Create a punch list of any remaining tasks, touch-ups, or corrections needed.

- Professional Inspection: Consider hiring a professional inspector to verify that all work meets building codes and quality standards.

- Final Walk-Through: Conduct a final walk-through with the contractor to ensure all work is completed to your satisfaction.

Handover Process:

- Documentation: Gather all relevant documentation, including warranties, manuals, and permits.

- Final Payments: Release final payments to contractors upon satisfactory completion of the project.

- Handover Checklist: Use a handover checklist to ensure all aspects of the project are complete and in order.

Permits and Regulations: Navigating Legal Requirements

Navigating the legal requirements for renovations is crucial to ensure compliance with local building codes and regulations. This section will discuss the importance of permits, the process for obtaining them, and how to stay compliant with regulations.

1. Understanding the Importance of Permits

Permits are required for various types of renovations to ensure the work complies with building codes and safety standards. Failing to obtain the necessary permits can result in fines, delays, and potential legal issues.

Reasons for Permits:

- Safety: Ensures the work is performed safely and meets all safety standards.

- Compliance: Verifies that the renovation complies with local building codes and regulations.

- Insurance: Helps maintain insurance coverage, as some policies may be void if work is done without permits.

- Resale Value: Ensures that future buyers can verify the work was done legally and to code.

2. Types of Permits

Different types of permits may be required depending on the scope and nature of the renovation project. Common Types of Permits:

- Building Permit: Required for structural changes, additions, and major renovations.

- Electrical Permit: Required for electrical work, such as rewiring, new installations, or upgrades.

- Plumbing Permit: Required for plumbing work, including new installations, repairs, or modifications.

- HVAC Permit: Required for heating, ventilation, and air conditioning installations or modifications.

- Demolition Permit: Required for demolishing existing structures or parts of structures.

3. The Permit Application Process

The process for obtaining permits varies by location but generally involves several key steps.

Steps to Obtain Permits:

- Research Requirements: Identify the permits required for your project based on local building codes and regulations.

- Prepare Documentation: Gather all necessary documentation, including plans, drawings, and specifications.

- Submit Application: Submit the permit application to the local building department or permitting authority.

- Review and Approval: The application will be reviewed by building officials, who may request additional information or modifications.

- Inspection Schedule: Once approved, schedule inspections at various stages of the project to ensure compliance with permit requirements.

- Final Approval: After all inspections are completed, obtain final approval and a certificate of occupancy (if applicable).

4. Staying Compliant with Regulations

Compliance with building codes and regulations is essential throughout the renovation process to avoid penalties and ensure the safety and quality of the work.

Key Compliance Strategies:

- Hire Licensed Professionals: Work with licensed contractors and tradespeople who are familiar with local codes and regulations.

- Follow Plans: Ensure all work is performed according to approved plans and specifications.

- Schedule Inspections: Schedule and pass all required inspections to verify compliance at each stage of the project.

- Keep Records: Maintain detailed records of all permits, inspections, and approvals.

5. Addressing Common Permit Issues

Navigating the permit process can present challenges. Understanding common issues and how to address them can help ensure a smoother process.
Common Permit Issues and Solutions:

- Application Denials: If your permit application is denied, review the reasons provided and make necessary revisions to address the concerns.

- Delays: To avoid delays, submit applications early and respond promptly to requests for additional information.

- Failed Inspections: If an inspection fails, address the issues identified by the inspector and schedule a re-inspection.

- Unpermitted Work: If unpermitted work is discovered, consult with a professional to determine the best course of action, which may include obtaining retroactive permits or correcting the work.

-

6. Legal and Financial Implications

Failing to obtain the necessary permits and comply with regulations can have significant legal and financial implications.
Potential Consequences:

- Fines and Penalties: Non-compliance can result in fines, penalties, and additional fees.

- Stop-Work Orders: Authorities may issue stop-work orders, halting the project until compliance is achieved.

- Increased Costs: Addressing non-compliance issues can result in additional costs for corrections, permits, and inspections.

- Liability: Unpermitted work can increase liability risks, especially if the work results in damage or injury.

7. Navigating Zoning and Land Use Regulations

In addition to building codes, renovations must comply with zoning and land use regulations that dictate how properties can be used and developed.

Key Zoning Considerations:

- Zoning Districts: Understand the zoning district of your property and the types of uses and structures permitted.

- Setbacks and Height Restrictions: Comply with setback requirements, which dictate the distance structures must be from property lines, and height restrictions that limit the height of buildings.

- Lot Coverage: Adhere to lot coverage regulations that limit the percentage of the property that can be covered by structures.

- Special Permits: Some projects may require special permits or variances to deviate from zoning regulations.

8. Working with Professionals for Permits and Regulations

Navigating permits and regulations can be complex, and working with professionals can help ensure compliance and streamline the process.

Key Professionals to Consult:

- Architects: Assist with design and ensure plans meet building codes and zoning regulations.

- Engineers: Provide structural, electrical, and mechanical expertise for complex projects.

- Permit Expediters: Professionals who specialize in navigating the permit process and can help expedite approvals.

- Real Estate Attorneys: Provide legal advice on compliance with building codes, zoning regulations, and other legal requirements.

Effective management of renovations involves detailed planning, careful coordination, and continuous monitoring to ensure projects are completed on time, within budget, and to a high standard of quality. Developing a comprehensive renovation plan, establishing realistic timelines, coordinating with contractors and suppliers, monitoring progress, and managing changes are all critical aspects of successful project management.

Navigating permits and regulations is equally important to ensure compliance with local building codes and zoning laws. Understanding the importance of permits, the types of permits required, the application process, and how to stay compliant with regulations can help avoid legal and financial pitfalls. Working with professionals such as architects, engineers, permit expediters, and real estate attorneys can further streamline the process and ensure your renovation projects are executed smoothly and successfully. By following these guidelines, you can effectively manage renovations and navigate legal requirements, ultimately enhancing the value and appeal of your real estate investments.

Chapter 7:

Renting Out Your Properties

Renting Out Your Properties

Renting out properties is a critical component of building a successful real estate portfolio. Effective management of rental properties involves setting competitive rental rates, marketing the properties to attract quality tenants, and thorough tenant screening to ensure reliability and compatibility. This section will delve into these aspects to provide a comprehensive guide on maximizing rental income and maintaining high occupancy rates.

Setting Rental Rates: Market Analysis and Pricing

Setting the right rental rate is crucial to attracting tenants and ensuring a steady income stream. Pricing too high can result in vacancies, while pricing too low can lead to lost revenue. Conducting a thorough market analysis and understanding various pricing strategies will help you set competitive rental rates.

1. Conducting Market Analysis

A comprehensive market analysis involves researching the local rental market to understand the current trends, demands, and rental prices for similar properties.

Steps to Conduct Market Analysis:

- Identify Comparable Properties:

    o Look for properties similar to yours in terms of size, location, amenities, and condition.

    o Use online rental platforms, local listings, and real estate websites to gather data.

- Analyze Rental Prices:

    o Compare the rental rates of these properties to get an idea of the going rates.

    o Note any variations based on specific features, such as renovated kitchens, extra bedrooms, or premium locations.

- Assess Occupancy Rates:

    o Investigate the occupancy rates in your area. High occupancy rates indicate strong demand and may justify higher rental rates.

    o Understand seasonal variations that might affect demand and pricing.

- Consider Market Trends:

    - Analyze trends in rental prices over time to identify patterns of increases or decreases.

    - Stay updated on local economic conditions, job market trends, and population growth, as these factors influence rental demand.

- Evaluate Neighborhood Factors:

    - Consider the amenities and services available in the neighborhood, such as schools, parks, public transportation, and shopping centers.

    - Assess the safety and overall appeal of the area, as these factors significantly impact rental prices.

2. Setting Competitive Rental Rates

After gathering and analyzing market data, set a rental rate that is competitive and aligns with your financial goals.

Strategies for Setting Rental Rates:

- Use Comparable Analysis:

    - Use the data from your market analysis to set a rental rate within the range of comparable properties.

- - Adjust the rate based on unique features or improvements that your property offers.

- Consider Operating Costs:

  - Calculate your operating costs, including mortgage payments, property taxes, insurance, maintenance, and management fees.

  - Ensure the rental rate covers these costs and provides a reasonable profit margin.

- Factor in Vacancy Rates:

  - Account for potential vacancies and ensure the rental rate compensates for periods when the property might be unoccupied.

  - A higher rental rate might be necessary to offset the risk of vacancies.

- Incorporate Amenities and Upgrades:

  - Highlight and price amenities and upgrades that add value to the property, such as new appliances, modern finishes, or additional services like lawn care or utilities included.

- Adjust for Seasonality:

- Be flexible with your rental rates to accommodate seasonal demand. Lower rates might be needed during off-peak seasons, while higher rates can be set during peak rental periods.

- Review and Adjust Regularly:
  - Regularly review your rental rates in response to changes in the market and your operating costs.
  - Adjust rates for new leases and renewals to ensure they remain competitive and profitable.

Marketing Your Rental: Strategies to Attract Tenants

Effective marketing is essential to attract quality tenants and minimize vacancies. A well-executed marketing strategy highlights the unique features of your property and reaches potential tenants through various channels.

1. Creating an Attractive Listing

An appealing and detailed listing is the cornerstone of your marketing efforts. It should provide all the necessary information and highlight the property's best features.

Key Elements of an Attractive Listing:

High-Quality Photos:

- Use high-resolution photos that showcase the property's interior and exterior.

    o Include pictures of each room, emphasizing clean and well-lit spaces.

    o Capture unique features and amenities, such as a renovated kitchen, backyard, or community facilities.

- Compelling Description:

    o Write a clear and engaging description that highlights the property's key features and benefits.

    o Mention any recent upgrades, energy-efficient appliances, or included services.

    o Describe the neighborhood, including nearby amenities, schools, and public transportation options.

- Detailed Information:

    o Provide comprehensive details, including the number of bedrooms and bathrooms, square footage, and available amenities.

- Specify lease terms, rental rates, security deposit requirements, and any additional fees.
- Include contact information and instructions for scheduling viewings or applying.

2. Utilizing Online Platforms

Online platforms are essential for reaching a broad audience and attracting potential tenants.
Popular Online Platforms:

- Real Estate Websites:
    - List your property on popular real estate websites such as Zillow, Realtor.com, and Trulia.
    - These platforms offer extensive reach and tools for managing inquiries and applications.
- Social Media:
    - Utilize social media platforms like Facebook, Instagram, and Twitter to market your rental property.
    - Join local community groups and real estate pages to share your listing.
- Rental Apps:

- Use rental-specific apps like Apartments.com, Rent.com, and HotPads to target prospective tenants actively searching for rentals.

- These apps often include features like virtual tours and tenant screening tools.

- Property Management Websites:

  - If you use a property management service, ensure your property is listed on their website.

  - Property management websites often attract high-quality tenants seeking professionally managed rentals.

3. Leveraging Traditional Marketing Methods

While online platforms are crucial, traditional marketing methods can also be effective, especially for local reach.

Traditional Marketing Strategies:

- For Rent Signs:

  - Place visible and attractive "For Rent" signs on the property to attract local traffic.

  - Include contact information and a brief description of the property.

- Flyers and Brochures:
    - Distribute flyers and brochures in local businesses, community centers, and bulletin boards.
    - Highlight key features and contact information.

- Local Newspapers and Magazines:
    - Advertise in local newspapers and community magazines to reach potential tenants who prefer traditional media.
    - Include a compelling photo and a brief description of the property.

- Networking and Referrals:
    - Leverage your personal and professional network to spread the word about your rental property.
    - Offer referral incentives to current tenants or colleagues who refer successful applicants.

Tenant Screening: Finding the Right Fit

Screening tenants is one of the most critical aspects of managing rental properties. Proper screening helps ensure you find reliable tenants who will pay rent on time, take care of the property, and adhere to lease terms.

1. Establishing Screening Criteria

Before beginning the screening process, establish clear and consistent criteria to evaluate potential tenants.

Key Screening Criteria:

- Income Verification:

    - Require proof of income, such as pay stubs, tax returns, or bank statements.

    - Ensure the tenant's income is at least 2.5 to 3 times the monthly rent to confirm affordability.

- Credit History:

    - Conduct a credit check to assess the tenant's financial responsibility.

    - Look for a reasonable credit score and review the credit report for any red flags, such as late payments, high debt, or bankruptcies.

- Rental History:

    - Verify the tenant's rental history by contacting previous landlords.

    - Inquire about their payment history, property care, and any issues during their tenancy.

- Background Check:
    - Perform a background check to identify any criminal history or legal issues.
    - Consider the nature and severity of any offenses and their relevance to tenancy.

- References:
    - Request personal and professional references to gain additional insights into the tenant's character and reliability.
    - Contact references to verify information and ask pertinent questions about the tenant's behavior and responsibility.

2. Implementing the Screening Process

A thorough and systematic screening process helps ensure you select the best tenant for your property.

Steps in the Screening Process:

- Application Form:
    - Provide a comprehensive rental application form that collects essential information, including employment details, rental history, income, and references.

- - Ensure the application includes a consent form for credit and background checks.

- Conduct Interviews:

    - Schedule interviews with potential tenants to discuss their application and assess their suitability.
    - Ask questions about their rental history, reasons for moving, and expectations for the new property.

- Verify Information:

    - Verify the information provided in the application, including employment, income, and rental history.
    - Contact references and previous landlords to confirm the tenant's background and reliability.

- Perform Checks:

    - Conduct credit, background, and eviction checks through reputable screening services.
    - Review the results carefully and consider any potential concerns.

- Evaluate Applications:

- Compare applications against your established criteria and select the tenant who best meets your requirements.
- Consider the overall profile, including income, credit history, rental history, and references.

3. Legal Considerations in Tenant Screening

Tenant screening must be conducted fairly and in compliance with legal requirements to avoid discrimination and legal issues.

Fair Housing Laws:

- Non-Discrimination:
    - Adhere to federal, state, and local fair housing laws that prohibit discrimination based on race, color, religion, sex, national origin, familial status, disability, and other protected characteristics.
    - Apply screening criteria consistently to all applicants to ensure fairness.

Privacy and Consent

- Obtaining Consent:
    - Ensure you obtain written consent from applicants before conducting credit and

background checks.

- o Clearly inform applicants about the purpose of these checks and how their information will be used.

- Handling Personal Information:

  - o Protect the privacy of applicants by securely storing their personal information and using it only for the intended purpose.

  - o Comply with applicable data protection laws and regulations to safeguard applicant information.

- Adverse Action Notices:

  - o If you decide not to rent to an applicant based on information obtained from a credit or background check, provide them with an adverse action notice.

  - o The notice should include the reason for the decision, the contact information of the reporting agency, and the applicant's right to dispute the information.

4. Making the Final Decision

After completing the screening process, carefully review all the information gathered to make an informed decision.

Steps to Finalize Tenant Selection:

- Compare Applicants:
    - Evaluate all qualified applicants against your screening criteria.
    - Consider factors such as income stability, creditworthiness, rental history, and references.

- Trust Your Instincts:
    - While data and criteria are important, also trust your instincts and impressions from interviews and interactions with applicants.

- Communicate Decision:
    - Notify the selected tenant promptly and provide clear instructions on the next steps, including lease signing and move-in arrangements.
    - Inform other applicants of your decision courteously and professionally.

Marketing Your Rental: Strategies to Attract Tenants

Effective marketing is essential to attract quality tenants and minimize vacancies. A well-executed marketing strategy highlights the unique features of your property and reaches potential tenants through various channels.

1. Creating an Attractive Listing

An appealing and detailed listing is the cornerstone of your marketing efforts. It should provide all the necessary information and highlight the property's best features.

Key Elements of an Attractive Listing:

- High-Quality Photos:
    - Use high-resolution photos that showcase the property's interior and exterior.
    - Include pictures of each room, emphasizing clean and well-lit spaces.
    - Capture unique features and amenities, such as a renovated kitchen, backyard, or community facilities.

- Compelling Description:
    - Write a clear and engaging description that highlights the property's key features and benefits.
    - Mention any recent upgrades, energy-efficient appliances, or included services.
    - Describe the neighborhood, including

nearby amenities, schools, and public transportation options.

- Detailed Information:

    o Provide comprehensive details, including the number of bedrooms and bathrooms, square footage, and available amenities.

    o Specify lease terms, rental rates, security deposit requirements, and any additional fees.

    o Include contact information and instructions for scheduling viewings or applying.

2. Utilizing Online Platforms

Online platforms are essential for reaching a broad audience and attracting potential tenants.

Popular Online Platforms:

- Real Estate Websites:

    o List your property on popular real estate websites such as Zillow, Realtor.com, and Trulia.

    o These platforms offer extensive reach and tools for managing inquiries and applications.

- Social Media:

    o Utilize social media platforms like Facebook, Instagram, and Twitter to market your rental property.

    o Join local community groups and real estate pages to share your listing.

- Rental Apps:

    o Use rental-specific apps like Apartments.com, Rent.com, and HotPads to target prospective tenants actively searching for rentals.

    o These apps often include features like virtual tours and tenant screening tools.

- Property Management Websites:

    o If you use a property management service, ensure your property is listed on their website.

    o Property management websites often attract high-quality tenants seeking professionally managed rentals.

3. Leveraging Traditional Marketing Methods

While online platforms are crucial, traditional marketing methods can also be effective, especially for local reach.

Traditional Marketing Strategies:

- For Rent Signs:

  - Place visible and attractive "For Rent" signs on the property to attract local traffic.

  - Include contact information and a brief description of the property.

- Flyers and Brochures:

  - Distribute flyers and brochures in local businesses, community centers, and bulletin boards.

  - Highlight key features and contact information.

- Local Newspapers and Magazines:

  - Advertise in local newspapers and community magazines to reach potential tenants who prefer traditional media.

  - Include a compelling photo and a brief description of the property.

- Networking and Referrals:

  - Leverage your personal and professional network to spread the word about your rental property.

- Offer referral incentives to current tenants or colleagues who refer successful applicants.

Tenant Screening: Finding the Right Fit

Screening tenants is one of the most critical aspects of managing rental properties. Proper screening helps ensure you find reliable tenants who will pay rent on time, take care of the property, and adhere to lease terms.

1. Establishing Screening Criteria

Before beginning the screening process, establish clear and consistent criteria to evaluate potential tenants.

Key Screening Criteria:

- Income Verification:
    - Require proof of income, such as pay stubs, tax returns, or bank statements.
    - Ensure the tenant's income is at least 2.5 to 3 times the monthly rent to confirm affordability.
- Credit History:
    - Conduct a credit check to assess the tenant's financial responsibility.
    - Look for a reasonable credit score and

review the credit report for any red flags, such as late payments, high debt, or bankruptcies.

- **Rental History:**
    - Verify the tenant's rental history by contacting previous landlords.
    - Inquire about their payment history, property care, and any issues during their tenancy.

- **Background Check:**
    - Perform a background check to identify any criminal history or legal issues.
    - Consider the nature and severity of any offenses and their relevance to tenancy.

- **References:**
    - Request personal and professional references to gain additional insights into the tenant's character and reliability.
    - Contact references to verify information and ask pertinent questions about the tenant's behavior and responsibility.

2. Implementing the Screening Process

A thorough and systematic screening process helps

ensure you select the best tenant for your property. Steps in the Screening Process:

Application Form:

- Provide a comprehensive rental application form that collects essential information, including employment details, rental history, income, and references.

    o Ensure the application includes a consent form for credit and background checks.

- Conduct Interviews:

    o Schedule interviews with potential tenants to discuss their application and assess their suitability.

    o Ask questions about their rental history, reasons for moving, and expectations for the new property.

- Verify Information:

    o Verify the information provided in the application, including employment, income, and rental history.

    o Contact references and previous landlords to confirm the tenant's background and reliability.

- Perform Checks:

- Conduct credit, background, and eviction checks through reputable screening services.

- Review the results carefully and consider any potential concerns.

- Evaluate Applications:

    - Compare applications against your established criteria and select the tenant who best meets your requirements.

    - Consider the overall profile, including income, credit history, rental history, and references.

3. Legal Considerations in Tenant Screening

Tenant screening must be conducted fairly and in compliance with legal requirements to avoid discrimination and legal issues.

Fair Housing Laws:

- Non-Discrimination:

    - Adhere to federal, state, and local fair housing laws that prohibit discrimination based on race, color, religion, sex, national origin, familial status, disability, and other protected characteristics.

- - Apply screening criteria consistently to all applicants to ensure fairness.

- Privacy and Consent:

  - Obtain written consent from applicants before conducting credit and background checks.

  - Clearly inform applicants about the purpose of these checks and how their information will be used.

- Handling Personal Information:

  - Protect the privacy of applicants by securely storing their personal information and using it only for the intended purpose.

  - Comply with applicable data protection laws and regulations to safeguard applicant information.

- Adverse Action Notices:

  - If you decide not to rent to an applicant based on information obtained from a credit or background check, provide them with an adverse action notice.

  - The notice should include the reason for the decision, the contact information of the reporting agency, and the applicant's right to dispute the information.

Making the Final Decision

After completing the screening process, carefully review all the information gathered to make an informed decision.

Steps to Finalize Tenant Selection:

- Compare Applicants:
    - Evaluate all qualified applicants against your screening criteria.
    - Consider factors such as income stability, creditworthiness, rental history, and references.

- Trust Your Instincts:
    - While data and criteria are important, also trust your instincts and impressions from interviews and interactions with applicants.

- Communicate Decision:
    - Notify the selected tenant promptly and provide clear instructions on the next steps, including lease signing and move-in arrangements.
    - Inform other applicants of your decision courteously and professionally.

Renting out your properties involves a multi-faceted approach to setting competitive rental rates, marketing effectively, and thoroughly screening tenants. By conducting a detailed market analysis and setting rental rates that reflect current market conditions, you can attract quality tenants while maximizing your rental income. Utilizing both online and traditional marketing methods ensures broad reach and visibility for your rental properties. Implementing a rigorous tenant screening process helps identify reliable tenants who will uphold lease terms and take good care of the property.

Adhering to legal requirements, protecting applicant privacy, and communicating clearly throughout the process are essential to maintaining fairness and avoiding potential legal issues. By following these guidelines, you can effectively manage your rental properties, maintain high occupancy rates, and build a successful real estate portfolio.

Lease Agreements: Key Terms and Conditions

A lease agreement is a legally binding contract between a landlord and a tenant that outlines the terms and conditions of the rental arrangement. Crafting a comprehensive and clear lease agreement is crucial to protect both parties' interests, minimize misunderstandings, and ensure a smooth landlord-tenant relationship. This section will cover the key terms and conditions that should be included in a lease agreement.

1. Essential Components of a Lease Agreement

Identifying Information

1.1 Parties Involved:

- Landlord Information: Include the landlord's full name, address, and contact details.

- Tenant Information: Include the tenant's full name, address, and contact details.

1.2 Property Details:

- Property Address: Clearly state the full address of the rental property, including the unit number (if applicable).

- Description: Provide a brief description of the property, such as the type of dwelling (e.g., apartment, single-family home, duplex).

2. Lease Term

2.1 Duration:

- Start Date: Specify the date the lease begins.

- End Date: Specify the date the lease ends.

- Fixed-Term Lease: A lease with a set duration, typically one year.

- Month-to-Month Lease: A lease that automatically renews each month until terminated by either party with proper notice.

3. Rent and Deposits

Rent Payments

3.1 Amount:

- Monthly Rent: Clearly state the amount of rent due each month.

3.2 Due Date:

- Payment Date: Specify the due date for rent payments (e.g., the first of each month).

3.3 Payment Methods:

- Accepted Methods: Outline acceptable payment methods (e.g., check, electronic transfer, credit card).

3.4 Late Fees:

- Late Payment Penalties: Specify any late fees and the grace period (if any) before a late fee is applied.

Security Deposits

3.5 Amount:

- Deposit Amount: State the amount of the security deposit required.

3.6 Use of Deposit:

- Purpose: Explain the purpose of the security deposit (e.g., covering damages, unpaid rent).

3.7 Return of Deposit:

- Return Conditions: Outline the conditions under which the deposit will be returned, including the timeframe and any deductions for damages or unpaid rent.

4. Maintenance and Repairs

Landlord Responsibilities

4.1 Property Maintenance:

- Repairs and Upkeep: Specify the landlord's responsibilities for maintaining the property and making necessary repairs.

4.2 Common Areas:

- Maintenance of Common Areas: Outline the landlord's duties related to common areas (if applicable).

Tenant Responsibilities

4.3 Tenant Maintenance:

- Tenant Obligations: State the tenant's responsibilities for keeping the property clean and reporting maintenance issues.

4.4 Reporting Issues:

- Maintenance Requests: Provide instructions for reporting maintenance issues and the expected response time.

5. Utilities and Services

Utility Payments

5.1 Tenant-Paid Utilities:

- Utilities Covered by Tenant: Specify which utilities the tenant is responsible for paying (e.g., electricity, gas, water).

5.2 Landlord-Paid Utilities:

- Utilities Covered by Landlord: Outline any utilities the landlord will cover (e.g., trash collection, sewage).

6. Rules and Regulations

Property Use

6.1 Occupancy Limits:

- Number of Occupants: State the maximum number of occupants allowed in the rental property.

6.2 Subletting:

- Subletting Policy: Specify whether subletting is allowed and any conditions or approval processes required.

6.3 Noise and Disturbances:

- Quiet Hours: Establish quiet hours and guidelines for noise levels to prevent disturbances to neighbors.

7. Entry and Access

Landlord Access

7.1 Notice Requirement:

- Entry Notice: Specify the notice period the landlord must provide before entering the rental property (e.g., 24 hours).

7.2 Permitted Reasons:

- Reasons for Entry: Outline the permitted reasons for landlord entry, such as inspections, repairs, or showing the property to prospective tenants.

8. Lease Termination

Termination Conditions

8.1 Early Termination:

- Conditions for Early Termination: Specify the conditions under which the lease may be terminated early by either party and any associated fees or penalties.

8.2 Notice Requirements:

- Notice Period: State the notice period required for termination by either party (e.g., 30 days).

8.3 Renewal Terms:

- Renewal Process: Outline the process for renewing the lease, including notice periods and any changes to terms or rent.

9. Legal Considerations

Compliance with Laws

9.1 Legal Compliance:

- Applicable Laws: Ensure the lease complies with local, state, and federal laws, including fair housing regulations.

9.2 Dispute Resolution:

- Dispute Resolution Process: Specify the process for resolving disputes, such as mediation or arbitration.

Move-In Process: Preparing Your Property for Tenants

The move-in process is a critical phase in rental property management. Properly preparing your property for new tenants ensures a smooth transition, sets the tone for a positive landlord-tenant relationship, and helps maintain the property's condition. This section will cover the steps to prepare your property for tenants and facilitate a seamless move-in experience.

1. Property Preparation

Cleaning and Repairs

1.1 Deep Cleaning:

- Thorough Cleaning: Conduct a thorough cleaning of the entire property, including floors, walls, windows, and appliances.

- Professional Services: Consider hiring professional cleaning services for a comprehensive and high-standard clean.

1.2 Maintenance and Repairs:

- Routine Maintenance: Perform routine maintenance tasks, such as changing HVAC filters, checking smoke detectors, and servicing appliances.

- Repairs: Address any necessary repairs, including

- plumbing, electrical, and structural issues, to ensure the property is in good condition.

Safety and Security

1.3 Security Measures:

- Locks and Keys: Change the locks and provide new keys to ensure security for the new tenants.

- Alarm Systems: Test and service any security systems, such as alarms or surveillance cameras.

1.4 Safety Compliance:

- Smoke Detectors and CO Alarms: Ensure smoke detectors and carbon monoxide alarms are installed and functioning properly.

- Fire Extinguishers: Provide fire extinguishers and ensure they are accessible and in good condition.

2. Documentation and Communication
Lease Agreement

2.1 Review Lease:

- Review and Sign: Review the lease agreement with the tenant, ensuring all terms and conditions are understood and agreed upon.

- Provide Copies: Provide a signed copy of the

lease agreement to the tenant and retain a copy for your records.

Move-In Inspection

2.2 Conduct Inspection:

- Walk-Through: Conduct a walk-through inspection with the tenant to document the property's condition at move-in.

- Inspection Report: Complete a move-in inspection report, noting any existing damage or issues, and have the tenant sign it.

Tenant Orientation

2.3 Property Orientation:

- Introduce Property Features: Show the tenant how to operate appliances, HVAC systems, and any other features of the property.

- Emergency Procedures: Explain emergency procedures, including the location of emergency exits, fire extinguishers, and contact information for emergency maintenance.

3. Utilities and Services

Utility Transfers

3.1 Utility Setup:

- Transfer Utilities: Ensure utilities are

transferred to the tenant's name or provide instructions for setting up new accounts.

- Utility Contact Information: Provide contact information for utility providers and any necessary account numbers.

Service Arrangements

3.2 Service Providers:

- Provide Contacts: Provide contact information for service providers, such as trash collection, pest control, and lawn care services.

- Service Schedules: Inform the tenant of service schedules and any related responsibilities.

4. Tenant Resources and Support

Welcome Packet

4.1 Welcome Packet:

- Essential Information: Provide a welcome packet containing essential information, such as contact numbers for maintenance, emergency services, and the landlord.

- Neighborhood Guide: Include a guide to the neighborhood, highlighting local amenities, shops, restaurants, and transportation options.

Tenant Portal

4.2 Online Access:

- Tenant Portal: If available, provide access to an online tenant portal for managing rent payments, maintenance requests, and communication.

- Instructions: Include instructions for using the portal and troubleshooting common issues.

5. Move-In Day Logistics

Coordination and Support

5.1 Move-In Schedule:

- Coordinate Move-In: Schedule and coordinate the move-in day with the tenant, ensuring a smooth transition.

- Provide Support: Offer assistance or recommendations for moving services, if needed.

5.2 Moving Day Assistance:

- On-Site Presence: Consider being present on move-in day to address any immediate concerns or questions.

- Welcome Gesture: Provide a small welcome gift or gesture, such as a plant or a list of local resources, to create a positive first impression.

A well-crafted lease agreement and a meticulously prepared move-in process are fundamental to successful property management. Lease agreements should include all essential terms and conditions, from rent payments and security deposits to maintenance responsibilities and legal compliance. Clear communication and thorough documentation help prevent misunderstandings and protect both parties' interests.

Preparing the property for new tenants involves comprehensive cleaning, necessary repairs, and ensuring safety measures are in place. Effective communication, including reviewing the lease agreement, conducting a move-in inspection, and providing a welcome packet, sets the stage for a positive landlord-tenant relationship. By following these guidelines, you can ensure a smooth move-in process and a successful tenancy, ultimately contributing to the long-term success of your rental property portfolio.

Chapter 8:

Property Management

Property Management

Managing rental properties effectively is crucial to maintaining their value, ensuring tenant satisfaction, and maximizing rental income. Property management encompasses a wide range of activities, from tenant interactions and rent collection to maintenance and legal compliance. This section explores the key aspects of property management, including self-management versus hiring a property manager, day-to-day operations, and maintenance and repairs.

Self-Management vs. Hiring a Manager: Weighing

Your Options

One of the first decisions a property owner must make is whether to manage the property themselves or hire a professional property manager. Both approaches have their advantages and disadvantages, and the right choice depends on various factors, including the owner's time, expertise, and resources.

Pros and Cons of Self-Management

Pros:

- Cost Savings:

  - No Management Fees: Self-management eliminates the cost of hiring a property manager, typically 8-12% of the monthly rent.

  - Direct Control: Owners have direct control over expenses and can make decisions without needing to consult a third party.

- Personal Investment:

  - Hands-On Approach: Owners can be directly involved in all aspects of property management, which can be rewarding and ensure that their standards are met.

  - Better Understanding: Managing the property personally provides a deeper understanding of its needs and tenant issues.

- Flexibility:

  - Customized Approach: Owners can tailor management practices to suit their preferences and the specific needs of the property and tenants.

Cons:

- Time-Consuming:
    - Daily Tasks: Managing a property requires a significant time commitment, including handling maintenance requests, collecting rent, and addressing tenant concerns.
    - 24/7 Availability: Owners must be available around the clock to respond to emergencies and urgent issues.

- Lack of Expertise:
    - Learning Curve: Owners without prior experience may face a steep learning curve and make mistakes that could be costly.
    - Legal Knowledge: Navigating landlord-tenant laws and regulations can be complex and requires a good understanding of legal requirements.

- Stress and Responsibility:
    - High Responsibility: Owners are responsible for all aspects of property management, which can be stressful and overwhelming, especially with multiple properties.

Pros and Cons of Hiring a Property Manager

Pros:

- Professional Expertise:

    o Experience: Property managers have the expertise and experience to handle all aspects of property management efficiently.

    o Legal Compliance: They are knowledgeable about landlord-tenant laws and regulations, ensuring compliance and reducing legal risks.

- Time Savings:
    o Delegation: Owners can delegate day-to-day management tasks, freeing up their time for other activities or investments.

    o 24/7 Availability: Property managers provide around-the-clock service, handling emergencies and urgent issues promptly.

- Tenant Management:

    o Screening and Selection: Property managers have established processes for tenant screening and selection, leading to higher-quality tenants.

    o Tenant Relations: They handle tenant interactions, including lease enforcement and conflict resolution.

Cons:

- Cost:

    o Management Fees: Hiring a property manager involves paying management fees, which can reduce overall rental income.

    o Additional Charges: Some property managers charge extra for specific services, such as leasing or maintenance coordination.

- Less Control:

    o Delegated Authority: Owners have less direct control over day-to-day management decisions and must rely on the property manager's judgment.

    o Potential Misalignment: There may be a misalignment of interests between the owner and the property manager.

- Finding the Right Manager:

    o Quality Variance: The quality of property management services can vary, and finding a reliable and competent manager requires careful research and vetting.

Making the Decision

To make an informed decision between self-management and hiring a property manager, consider the following factors:

- Number of Properties:

    o Managing a single property might be feasible for many owners, but as the number of properties increases, the complexity and time required for management also increase.

- Proximity to Properties:

    o If you live close to your rental properties, self-management might be more practical. However, if the properties are located far away, hiring a property manager can save time and travel expenses.

- Time Availability:

    o Consider how much time you can realistically dedicate to property management. If you have a full-time job or other commitments, hiring a property manager might be the best option.

- Experience and Expertise:

    o Assess your knowledge and experience in property management. If you lack expertise in areas such as legal compliance, maintenance, or tenant relations, a professional manager can provide valuable support.

- Financial Considerations:
    - Weigh the cost of property management fees against the potential benefits of professional management, such as higher tenant retention rates and fewer legal issues.

Day-to-Day Operations: Routine Tasks and Responsibilities

Effective property management involves a range of routine tasks and responsibilities that ensure the smooth operation of the property and satisfaction of tenants.

Rent Collection and Financial Management

Rent Collection:

- Due Dates: Ensure tenants are aware of rent due dates and the accepted payment methods.

- Late Fees: Implement and enforce late fees for overdue rent payments to encourage timely payments.

- Record Keeping: Maintain accurate records of rent payments and any outstanding balances.

Financial Management:

- Budgeting: Create and manage a budget for the property, accounting for all income and expenses.

- Expense Tracking: Track and categorize all property-related expenses, including maintenance, utilities, and management fees.

- Reporting: Generate regular financial reports to monitor the property's financial performance.

Tenant Relations and Communication

Tenant Communication:

- Availability: Be accessible to tenants for questions, concerns, and maintenance requests.

- Regular Updates: Provide regular updates to tenants on property-related matters, such as scheduled maintenance or policy changes.

- Conflict Resolution: Address and resolve tenant disputes and conflicts promptly and fairly.

Lease Enforcement:

- Lease Compliance: Ensure tenants adhere to the terms and conditions of their lease agreements.

- Notices: Issue notices for lease violations, such as late payments or unauthorized pets, and follow up on compliance.

- Evictions: Handle the eviction process if necessary, following legal procedures and timelines.

Maintenance and Repairs

Routine Maintenance:

- Scheduled Inspections: Conduct regular inspections of the property to identify and address maintenance issues early.

- Preventive Maintenance: Implement preventive maintenance practices to reduce the likelihood of major repairs, such as servicing HVAC systems and cleaning gutters.

- Seasonal Tasks: Perform seasonal maintenance tasks, such as winterizing plumbing and landscaping.

Repairs:

- Timely Response: Respond promptly to repair requests to maintain tenant satisfaction and prevent further damage.

- Vendor Coordination: Coordinate with contractors and vendors for repairs and maintenance work, ensuring quality and timely completion.

- Expense Management: Track repair expenses and ensure they are within the budget.

Legal and Administrative Duties

Lease Management:

- Lease Renewals: Manage lease renewals and negotiate new lease terms with existing tenants.

- Lease Documentation: Maintain accurate lease documentation and ensure all leases are up to date.

Regulatory Compliance:

- Fair Housing Laws: Ensure compliance with fair housing laws and regulations to avoid discrimination claims.

- Building Codes: Adhere to local building codes and safety regulations, including fire safety and accessibility standards.

Record Keeping:

- Tenant Records: Maintain detailed records of tenant applications, leases, correspondence, and maintenance requests.

- Financial Records: Keep comprehensive financial records, including income, expenses, and tax documents.

Maintenance and Repairs: Keeping Your Property in Top Shape

Maintaining the property in good condition is essential for tenant satisfaction, preserving property value, and minimizing costly repairs. A proactive approach to maintenance and repairs helps achieve these goals.

Routine and Preventive Maintenance

Routine Maintenance:

- Regular Inspections: Conduct regular inspections of the property, including common areas, to identify and address maintenance needs.

- Cleaning: Ensure common areas, such as hallways and lobbies, are cleaned regularly to maintain a pleasant living environment.

- Landscaping: Maintain the property's landscaping, including mowing lawns, trimming bushes, and cleaning walkways.

Preventive Maintenance:

- HVAC Systems: Schedule regular servicing of heating, ventilation, and air conditioning systems to ensure efficient operation and prevent breakdowns.

- Plumbing: Inspect plumbing systems for leaks, clogs, and other issues, and perform routine maintenance, such as flushing water heaters.

- Roof and Gutters: Inspect and clean gutters regularly to prevent water damage and ensure the roof is in good condition.

Handling Repairs

Minor Repairs:

- Quick Fixes: Address minor repairs promptly, such as fixing leaky faucets, replacing light bulbs, and repairing door handles.

- In-House Maintenance: If feasible, have an in-house maintenance person handle minor repairs to save on costs and ensure quick response times.

Major Repairs:

- Professional Contractors: Hire professional contractors for major repairs, such as electrical work, plumbing, and structural repairs, to ensure quality and compliance with codes.

- Quotes and Bids: Obtain multiple quotes or bids for major repair projects to ensure competitive pricing and quality workmanship.

- Project Management: Oversee major repair projects to ensure they are completed on time and within budget, and address any issues that arise during the process.

Emergency Repairs

Emergency Protocols:

- Contact Information: Provide tenants with emergency contact information for after-hours repairs.

- Immediate Response: Respond to emergency repair requests, such as water leaks, electrical failures, and heating system breakdowns, immediately to prevent further damage and ensure tenant safety.

Vendor Relationships:

- Trusted Vendors: Establish relationships with trusted vendors and contractors who can respond quickly to emergency repair needs.

- Service Agreements: Consider service agreements with vendors for priority response and regular maintenance services.

Long-Term Maintenance Planning

Capital Improvements:

- Upgrade Planning: Plan for long-term capital improvements, such as roof replacements, HVAC upgrades, and major renovations, to maintain the property's value and appeal.

- Budgeting: Budget for capital improvements by setting aside funds each year based on the property's age and condition.

Asset Management:

- Lifecycle Management: Track the lifecycle of major systems and components, such as roofs, HVAC systems, and appliances, to anticipate replacement needs.

- Reserve Fund: Maintain a reserve fund to cover unexpected repairs and replacements without impacting the property's cash flow.

Property management is a multifaceted responsibility that requires a balance of skills, time, and resources. Deciding between self-management and hiring a property manager involves weighing the pros and cons of each approach based on factors such as cost, control, time commitment, and expertise. Both self-management and professional management have their advantages and disadvantages, and the best choice depends on the specific circumstances and goals of the property owner.

Effective property management encompasses a wide range of daily operations, from rent collection and tenant relations to maintenance and legal compliance. Ensuring that these tasks are handled efficiently and professionally is crucial for maintaining tenant satisfaction, preserving property value, and maximizing rental income. By implementing proactive maintenance and repair strategies, property owners can keep their properties in top shape, minimize costly repairs, and enhance tenant retention. Ultimately, successful property management contributes to the long-term success and profitability of a rental property portfolio.

Handling Tenant Issues: Communication and Problem Solving

Effective communication and problem-solving skills are crucial in property management. Handling tenant issues promptly and professionally can lead to higher tenant satisfaction, reduced turnover, and overall smoother management operations. This section will explore strategies for effective communication, common tenant issues, and methods for resolving conflicts.

1. The Importance of Effective Communication Building Relationships

Effective communication is the foundation of a positive landlord-tenant relationship. By establishing clear lines of communication from the beginning, you can build trust and foster a cooperative atmosphere.

Key Strategies:

- Open Dialogue: Encourage open dialogue with tenants and be approachable.

- Regular Updates: Keep tenants informed about important property-related information, such as maintenance schedules and policy changes.

- Prompt Responses: Respond to tenant inquiries and concerns promptly to demonstrate that you value their issues.

Setting Expectations

Clear communication about policies, procedures, and expectations can prevent misunderstandings and disputes.

Key Strategies:

- Welcome Packet: Provide a welcome packet that outlines property rules, contact information, and emergency procedures.

- Lease Agreement: Ensure the lease agreement clearly states all terms and conditions.

- Orientation: Conduct a move-in orientation to review key points and address any questions.

2. Common Tenant Issues and How to Address Them
Maintenance Requests

Maintenance issues are among the most common tenant concerns. Addressing these promptly is essential for tenant satisfaction and property upkeep.

Key Strategies:

- Maintenance Requests: Implement an easy-to-use system for tenants to submit maintenance requests.

- Response Time: Establish and communicate expected response times for different types of maintenance issues.

- Preventive Maintenance: Conduct regular inspections and preventive maintenance to reduce the occurrence of issues.

Noise Complaints

Noise complaints can disrupt the peace and lead to conflicts between tenants.

Key Strategies:

- Quiet Hours: Establish and enforce quiet hours to minimize noise disturbances.

- Mediation: Mediate between tenants if noise complaints arise and seek a mutually agreeable solution.

- Soundproofing: Consider soundproofing measures for properties with frequent noise issues.

Rent Payment Issues

Late or missed rent payments can impact cash flow and lead to legal action if not addressed.

Key Strategies:

- Clear Policies: Clearly outline rent payment

due dates, accepted payment methods, and late fees in the lease agreement.

- Reminders: Send rent reminders before the due date to encourage timely payments.

- Payment Plans: Offer payment plans for tenants facing temporary financial difficulties.

Pet Complaints

Pets can be a source of disputes due to noise, damage, or allergies.

Key Strategies:

- Pet Policy: Clearly outline the pet policy in the lease agreement, including any restrictions and fees.

- Damage Inspections: Conduct regular inspections to assess and address any pet-related damage.

- Pet Agreement: Have tenants sign a separate pet agreement detailing their responsibilities.

3. Conflict Resolution and Problem-Solving
Active Listening

Active listening is essential for understanding tenant concerns and finding effective solutions.

Key Strategies:

- Listen Carefully: Give tenants your full attention when they express concerns.

- Ask Questions: Clarify details by asking questions and summarizing what the tenant has said.

- Empathy: Show empathy and understanding, even if you do not agree with the tenant's perspective.

Negotiation

Effective negotiation skills can help resolve conflicts amicably and prevent escalation.

Key Strategies:

- Compromise: Look for win-win solutions that address both parties' needs.

- Flexibility: Be willing to adjust policies or make exceptions when reasonable.

- Document Agreements: Ensure that any agreed-upon solutions are documented and signed by both parties.

Legal Considerations

Understanding and adhering to legal requirements is crucial when handling tenant issues.

Key Strategies:

- Know the Law: Familiarize yourself with local landlord-tenant laws and regulations.

- Fair Housing: Ensure compliance with fair housing laws to avoid discrimination claims.

- Documentation: Keep detailed records of all communications and actions taken to address tenant issues.

Rent Collection and Accounting: Efficient Systems and Tools

Efficient rent collection and accounting practices are essential for maintaining cash flow, ensuring financial stability, and simplifying tax reporting. This section will cover effective systems and tools for rent collection, accounting best practices, and financial management strategies.

1. Rent Collection Methods

Traditional Methods

Traditional rent collection methods include cash, checks, and money orders. While these methods are still in use, they come with certain limitations.

Pros:

- No Transaction Fees: Cash, checks, and money orders do not incur transaction fees.

- Familiarity: Many tenants are familiar with these methods and may prefer them.

Cons:

- Security Risks: Handling cash and checks carries security risks, such as theft or loss.

- Manual Processing: These methods require manual processing, which can be time-consuming and prone to errors.

- Delayed Payments: Checks can take several days to clear, leading to delays in fund availability.

Electronic Payments

Electronic payment methods offer greater convenience and efficiency for both landlords and tenants.

Pros:

- Convenience: Tenants can make payments easily and securely from anywhere.

- Automatic Payments: Electronic systems can automate recurring payments, reducing the risk of late payments.

- Real-Time Processing: Payments are processed in real time, improving cash flow.

Cons:

- Transaction Fees: Some electronic payment systems charge transaction fees.

- Technical Issues: Electronic systems can experience technical issues or downtime.

- Common Electronic Payment Methods:

- Online Portals: Many property management software platforms offer online payment portals for tenants.

- Direct Deposit: Tenants can set up direct deposit payments directly to the landlord's bank account.

- Mobile Payment Apps: Apps like Venmo, PayPal, and Zelle offer convenient mobile payment options.

2. Implementing Efficient Accounting Systems Property Management Software

Property management software streamlines rent collection, accounting, and financial reporting.

Key Features:

- Automated Rent Collection: Automate rent collection through online portals and recurring payment setups.

- Expense Tracking: Track property-related

expenses, including maintenance, utilities, and management fees.

- Financial Reporting: Generate detailed financial reports, such as income statements, balance sheets, and cash flow statements.

- Tenant Management: Manage tenant information, lease agreements, and communication in one platform.

Popular Property Management Software:

- AppFolio: A comprehensive platform for rent collection, accounting, and tenant management.

- Buildium: Offers features for online payments, maintenance tracking, and financial reporting.

- Rentec Direct: Provides tools for rent collection, expense tracking, and tenant screening.

Bookkeeping Practices

Maintaining accurate and organized financial records is essential for effective property management.

Best Practices:

- Separate Accounts: Maintain separate bank accounts for personal and property-related finances to simplify accounting.

- Regular Reconciliation: Reconcile bank statements regularly to ensure accuracy and identify discrepancies.

- Detailed Records: Keep detailed records of all financial transactions, including rent payments, expenses, and deposits.

- Tax Documentation: Organize and store all tax-related documents, such as receipts, invoices, and financial statements, for easy access during tax season.

3. Financial Management Strategies

Budgeting

Creating and managing a budget helps ensure financial stability and plan for future expenses.

Key Components:

- Income Projections: Estimate rental income based on current leases and occupancy rates.

- Expense Forecasting: Project property-related expenses, including maintenance, utilities, taxes, and management fees.

- Cash Flow Management: Monitor cash flow to ensure sufficient funds are available for ongoing expenses and unexpected repairs.

Reserve Funds

Maintaining reserve funds provides financial security for unexpected expenses and capital improvements.

Key Strategies:

- Emergency Fund: Set aside funds for unexpected repairs, such as plumbing or HVAC issues.

- Capital Improvement Fund: Save for long-term capital improvements, such as roof replacements or major renovations.

- Regular Contributions: Make regular contributions to reserve funds to build a financial cushion over time.

Tax Planning

Effective tax planning can help minimize tax liabilities and ensure compliance with tax regulations.

Key Strategies:

- Deductible Expenses: Identify and track deductible expenses, such as mortgage interest, property taxes, and maintenance costs.

- Depreciation: Take advantage of depreciation deductions for rental properties to reduce taxable income.

- Professional Advice: Consult with a tax

professional to ensure accurate tax reporting and identify potential tax-saving opportunities.

Effective property management requires a combination of strong communication skills, efficient systems, and proactive problem-solving strategies. By handling tenant issues promptly and professionally, property owners can maintain positive relationships, reduce turnover, and ensure a well-managed property.

Implementing efficient rent collection and accounting practices is essential for maintaining financial stability and simplifying tax reporting. Utilizing property management software, maintaining accurate financial records, and adopting sound financial management strategies can help property owners optimize their operations and achieve long-term success.

By following these guidelines, property owners can effectively manage their rental properties, enhance tenant satisfaction, and maximize rental income, ultimately contributing to the success and growth of their real estate portfolio.

Chapter 9:

Scaling Your Portfolio

Scaling Your Portfolio

Scaling your real estate portfolio involves strategic planning, financial readiness, and market knowledge. It is a crucial step toward achieving greater financial success and diversification. This section covers key aspects of scaling your portfolio, including recognizing when to expand, financing additional properties, and diversifying your investments.

When to Expand: Indicators You're Ready to Grow

Expanding your real estate portfolio is a significant decision that requires careful consideration and planning. Several indicators can help you determine whether you are ready to take this step.

1. Strong Financial Position

A robust financial foundation is essential for scaling your portfolio. Assess your current financial situation to ensure you have the stability and resources needed to invest in additional properties.

Key Indicators:

- Positive Cash Flow: Your existing properties generate consistent positive cash flow, covering expenses and providing profit.

- Emergency Fund: You have an adequate emergency fund to cover unexpected expenses for your current properties.

- Debt Management: Your current debt levels are manageable, and you have a good credit score.

2. Market Knowledge and Experience

Experience and knowledge of the real estate market are critical for successful expansion. Ensure you have a solid understanding of market trends, property management, and investment strategies.

Key Indicators:

- Track Record: You have a proven track record of successful property management and investment.

- Market Research: You regularly conduct market research and stay informed about real estate trends and economic conditions.

- Networking: You have a network of industry professionals, such as real estate agents, lenders, and contractors, to support your expansion.

3. Clear Investment Strategy

A well-defined investment strategy helps guide your expansion and ensures your new investments align with your overall goals.

Key Indicators:

- Defined Goals: You have clear short-term and long-term investment goals.

- Risk Tolerance: You understand your risk tolerance and have strategies in place to mitigate risks.

- Diversification Plan: You have a plan for diversifying your portfolio to spread risk and maximize returns.

4. Time and Resource Availability

Expanding your portfolio requires time and resources. Assess whether you can commit the necessary time and resources to manage additional properties effectively.

Key Indicators:

- Time Commitment: You have the time to dedicate to managing new properties or the resources to hire additional support.

- Support Systems: You have established support systems, such as property management services, to assist with the increased workload.

Financing Additional Properties: Strategies for Scaling

Securing financing is a critical step in expanding your real estate portfolio. Various financing strategies can help you acquire additional properties and manage your cash flow effectively.

1. Traditional Mortgages

Traditional mortgages are a common financing option for purchasing additional properties. They offer competitive interest rates and fixed payment terms.

Key Considerations:

- Credit Score: Ensure your credit score is strong to qualify for favorable mortgage terms.

- Down Payment: Be prepared to make a substantial down payment, typically 20% of the property's purchase price.

- Debt-to-Income Ratio: Maintain a healthy debt-to-income ratio to improve your chances of approval.

2. Home Equity Loans and HELOCs

Home equity loans and home equity lines of credit (HELOCs) allow you to leverage the equity in your existing properties to finance additional investments.

Key Considerations:

- Equity: Calculate the available equity in your current properties to determine your borrowing capacity.

- Interest Rates: Compare interest rates and terms for home equity loans and HELOCs.

- Repayment Terms: Understand the repayment terms and how they will impact your cash flow.

3. Private Lenders

Private lenders can offer more flexible financing options compared to traditional banks. They may be willing to finance properties that do not meet conventional lending criteria.

Key Considerations:

- Interest Rates: Private lenders often charge higher interest rates than traditional banks.

- Terms and Conditions: Carefully review the terms and conditions of the loan, including fees and repayment schedules.

- Reputation: Work with reputable private lenders to avoid predatory lending practices.

4. Partnerships and Joint Ventures

Forming partnerships or joint ventures can provide additional capital and resources for acquiring new properties. This strategy allows you to share the risks and rewards with other investors.

Key Considerations:

- Partnership Agreement: Clearly define the roles, responsibilities, and profit-sharing arrangements in a written partnership agreement.

- Due Diligence: Conduct thorough due diligence on potential partners to ensure compatibility and trustworthiness.

- Exit Strategy: Establish an exit strategy to address how the partnership will be dissolved or how partners can exit the investment.

5. Seller Financing

Seller financing, also known as owner financing, allows you to purchase a property directly from the seller without traditional bank financing. The seller acts as the lender and provides financing terms.

Key Considerations:

- Negotiation: Negotiate favorable terms with the seller, including interest rates, repayment schedules, and down payments.

- Legal Considerations: Ensure all terms are documented in a legally binding contract.

- Creditworthiness: Demonstrate your

creditworthiness to the seller to secure better terms.

6. Cash Purchases

If you have substantial liquid assets, purchasing properties with cash can offer significant advantages, such as faster transactions and no interest payments.

Key Considerations:

- Liquidity: Ensure you have sufficient liquidity to cover the purchase price and any additional expenses.

- Investment Diversification: Avoid tying up all your capital in a single property to maintain diversification.

- Opportunity Cost: Consider the opportunity cost of using cash for property purchases versus other investment opportunities.

Diversifying Your Investments: Types of Properties and Markets

Diversification is a key strategy for managing risk and maximizing returns in your real estate portfolio. By investing in different types of properties and markets, you can spread risk and take advantage of various growth opportunities.

1. Types of Properties

Diversifying your portfolio with different types of

properties can provide stability and multiple income streams.

Residential Properties:

- Single-Family Homes: Ideal for long-term rentals and can attract stable, long-term tenants.

- Multi-Family Properties: Offer higher rental income and lower vacancy risk due to multiple units.

- Condos and Townhouses: Require less maintenance but may have homeowners association (HOA) fees and regulations.

Commercial Properties:

- Office Buildings: Provide higher rental income but can be sensitive to economic downturns.

- Retail Spaces: Can offer stable returns if located in high-traffic areas but may be affected by e-commerce trends.

- Industrial Properties: Include warehouses and manufacturing facilities, often with long-term leases and lower vacancy rates.

Specialty Properties:

- Vacation Rentals: Generate high rental income during peak seasons but may have higher vacancy rates off-season.

- Student Housing: Located near universities, these properties offer high demand but may require more maintenance.

- Senior Living Facilities: Benefit from an aging population and provide stable, long-term income.

2. Market Diversification

Investing in different geographic markets can reduce the impact of local economic fluctuations and provide access to diverse growth opportunities.

Local Markets:

- Familiarity: Investing in your local market allows for easier management and better understanding of market conditions.

- Networking: Leverage local networks and relationships with real estate agents, contractors, and other professionals.

Regional Markets:

- Economic Diversity: Regional markets can offer economic diversity and resilience against localized downturns.

- Growth Potential: Identify regions with strong population growth, job creation, and infrastructure development.

- National and International Markets:

- Broader Opportunities: Investing nationally or internationally provides access to a wider range of opportunities and can enhance portfolio diversification.

- Currency and Political Risks: Consider currency exchange rates, political stability, and legal regulations when investing in international markets.

3. Risk Management and Due Diligence

Proper risk management and due diligence are essential when scaling your portfolio. By thoroughly evaluating each investment, you can minimize risks and make informed decisions.

Risk Management Strategies

Market Analysis:

- Economic Indicators: Monitor key economic indicators, such as employment rates, GDP growth, and real estate trends, to assess market conditions.

- Supply and Demand: Analyze supply and demand dynamics in the target market to identify potential risks and opportunities.

Property Evaluation:

- Physical Condition: Conduct thorough

inspections to assess the property's condition and identify potential maintenance issues.

- Location: Evaluate the property's location in terms of accessibility, amenities, and future growth potential.

- Tenant Profile: Understand the target tenant profile and assess the demand for rental properties in the area.

Financial Analysis:

- Cash Flow Projections: Create detailed cash flow projections to evaluate the property's potential income and expenses.

- Break-Even Analysis: Determine the break-even point to understand the property's financial viability.

- Return on Investment (ROI): Calculate the expected ROI to assess the property's profitability.

Due Diligence Process

Legal Review:

- Title Search: Conduct a title search to ensure there are no liens or legal issues with the property.

- Zoning and Permits: Verify that the property complies with zoning regulations and has all necessary permits.

- Environmental Assessment:

  - Environmental Risks: Assess environmental risks, such as flood zones, soil contamination, and asbestos, to identify potential liabilities.

  - Mitigation Measures: Implement mitigation measures to address any identified environmental risks.

Tenant Verification:

- Lease Agreements: Review existing lease agreements to understand the terms and conditions, including rental rates and lease duration.

- Tenant Background Checks: Conduct background checks on existing tenants to assess their reliability and payment history.

4. Implementing a Scaling Strategy

Implementing a scaling strategy involves careful planning, resource allocation, and ongoing management. By following a structured approach, you can achieve sustainable growth and maximize returns.

Strategic Planning

Goal Setting:

- Short-Term Goals: Define specific, measurable

short-term goals, such as acquiring a certain number of properties within a year.

- Long-Term Goals: Establish long-term goals, such as reaching a target portfolio size or achieving a specific level of passive income.

Timeline:

- Phased Approach: Implement a phased approach to scaling, allowing for adjustments and reassessment at each stage.

- Milestones: Set milestones to track progress and make necessary adjustments to your strategy.

Resource Allocation

Financial Resources:

- Budgeting: Allocate a budget for property acquisitions, maintenance, and other expenses.

- Financing: Secure financing for additional properties through traditional mortgages, home equity loans, private lenders, or partnerships.

Human Resources:

- Team Building: Build a team of professionals, including real estate agents, property managers, contractors, and legal advisors, to support your expansion.

- Delegation: Delegate tasks to team members to ensure efficient management and focus on strategic decisions.

Property Acquisition

Market Research:

- Target Markets: Identify target markets based on economic indicators, growth potential, and investment opportunities.

- Property Selection: Select properties that align with your investment strategy and have strong potential for appreciation and rental income.

Due Diligence:

- Inspections: Conduct thorough inspections to assess the property's condition and identify any issues.

- Financial Analysis: Perform detailed financial analysis to evaluate the property's cash flow, ROI, and break-even point.

Negotiation:

- Offer: Make competitive offers based on market value and financial analysis.

- Terms: Negotiate favorable terms, including purchase price, contingencies, and closing costs.

5. Ongoing Management and Monitoring

Effective ongoing management and monitoring are crucial for ensuring the success of your expanded portfolio. Regularly review and adjust your strategies to maintain optimal performance.

Property Management

Day-to-Day Operations:

- Rent Collection: Implement efficient rent collection systems to ensure timely payments.

- Maintenance: Conduct regular maintenance and address repair requests promptly to maintain property condition and tenant satisfaction.

Tenant Relations:

- Communication: Maintain open lines of communication with tenants to address concerns and build positive relationships.

- Lease Management: Manage lease renewals, terminations, and compliance with lease terms.

Financial Monitoring

Cash Flow Management:

- Expense Tracking: Monitor and track all property-related expenses to manage cash flow effectively.

- Budgeting: Adjust budgets based on actual performance and forecast future expenses.

Performance Analysis:

- KPIs: Track key performance indicators (KPIs), such as occupancy rates, rental income, and ROI, to assess the performance of your properties.

- Reporting: Generate regular financial reports to review portfolio performance and make data-driven decisions.

Scaling your real estate portfolio is a strategic process that requires careful planning, financial readiness, and ongoing management. By recognizing the indicators that you are ready to expand, exploring various financing options, and diversifying your investments, you can achieve sustainable growth and maximize returns. Implementing a structured approach to scaling, including strategic planning, resource allocation, and effective management, will help you build a successful and diversified real estate portfolio. By following these guidelines, you can navigate the complexities of scaling your portfolio and achieve long-term success in the real estate market.

Leveraging Equity: Using Existing Properties to

Finance New Ones

Leveraging the equity in your existing properties can be an effective strategy to finance new acquisitions, allowing you to grow your portfolio without requiring substantial upfront capital. Understanding the various methods of leveraging equity and their implications is crucial for successful scaling.

Understanding Home Equity

Home equity is the difference between the market value of your property and the outstanding balance on your mortgage. For example, if your property is worth $300,000 and you owe $200,000 on your mortgage, you have $100,000 in equity.

Key Concepts:

- Loan-to-Value Ratio (LTV): The LTV ratio is a measure of how much equity you have in your property. It is calculated by dividing the mortgage balance by the property's market value. A lower LTV indicates more equity.

- Equity Build-Up: Equity increases as you pay down your mortgage and as the property's market value appreciates.

Methods for Leveraging Equity

1. Cash-Out Refinance

Cash-out refinancing involves replacing your existing mortgage with a new, larger mortgage. The difference between the new loan amount and the existing mortgage balance is provided to you in cash, which can be used to finance new investments.

Advantages:

- Lower Interest Rates: Refinance rates are typically lower than other forms of borrowing, reducing your overall borrowing costs.

- Single Loan Payment: Consolidates your mortgage into a single monthly payment.

Disadvantages:

- Closing Costs: Refinancing involves closing costs, which can be significant.

- Increased Debt: Increases your mortgage balance, which can affect your debt-to-income ratio.

Example:

Current Mortgage Balance: $200,000
Property Value: $300,000
New Loan Amount: $250,000
Cash-Out Amount: $50,000 (minus closing costs)

2. Home Equity Loan

A home equity loan, also known as a second mortgage, allows you to borrow a lump sum based on your equity. This loan is separate from your primary mortgage and typically has a fixed interest rate.

Advantages:

- Fixed Interest Rate: Provides predictable monthly payments.

- Lump Sum: Receive a lump sum, which can be used for large investments.

Disadvantages:

- Second Loan: Adds an additional monthly payment on top of your existing mortgage.

- Interest Costs: Higher interest rates compared to primary mortgages.

Example:

Equity: $100,000
Loan Amount: Up to 80% of equity, or $80,000

3. Home Equity Line of Credit (HELOC)

A HELOC provides a revolving line of credit based on your home equity, similar to a credit card. You can draw funds as needed during the draw period, and repay them during the repayment period.

Advantages:

- Flexibility: Draw funds as needed, up to your credit limit.

- Interest-Only Payments: During the draw period, you may only need to make interest payments.

- Disadvantages:

- Variable Interest Rates: Rates can fluctuate, affecting your monthly payments.

- Risk of Over-Borrowing: Easy access to funds can lead to over-borrowing.

Example:

Equity: $100,000
HELOC Limit: Up to 85% of equity, or $85,000

Steps to Leverage Equity for New Investments

1. Assess Your Equity

Calculate the available equity in your existing properties by estimating their current market value and subtracting the outstanding mortgage balances. Use professional appraisals for accurate valuations.

2. Choose the Right Financing Option

Evaluate the different methods for leveraging equity and choose the one that best fits your financial situation and investment goals. Consider factors such as interest rates, repayment terms, and the impact on your overall debt.

3. Prepare Financial Documentation

Gather all necessary financial documentation,

including recent property appraisals, mortgage statements, tax returns, and proof of income. Lenders will require this information to assess your eligibility and determine loan terms.

4. Apply for Financing

Submit applications for the chosen financing option(s) and negotiate terms with lenders. Be prepared to provide additional information or clarification as requested.

5. Use Funds Strategically

Once approved, use the funds strategically to acquire new properties that align with your investment goals. Conduct thorough due diligence on potential acquisitions to ensure they offer strong potential for appreciation and rental income.

6. Monitor and Adjust

Regularly review your financial situation and the performance of your investments. Adjust your strategy as needed to maintain a healthy balance between debt and equity, and to optimize your portfolio's growth.

Managing a Larger Portfolio: Systems and Processes

As your real estate portfolio grows, effective management becomes increasingly important. Implementing robust systems and processes can help you streamline operations, maintain tenant satisfaction, and maximize returns.

Property Management Systems

1. Property Management Software

Investing in property management software can significantly enhance your ability to manage multiple properties efficiently. These platforms offer a range of features, including rent collection, maintenance tracking, and financial reporting.

Key Features:

- Automated Rent Collection: Streamline rent collection through online portals and automated reminders.

- Maintenance Management: Track maintenance requests, schedule repairs, and monitor completion.
- Tenant Communication: Centralize communication with tenants through messaging systems and portals.

- Financial Reporting: Generate detailed financial reports, including income statements, balance sheets, and cash flow statements.

Popular Property Management Software:

- AppFolio: Comprehensive platform for rent collection, accounting, and tenant management.

- Buildium: Offers features for online payments, maintenance tracking, and financial reporting.

- Rentec Direct: Provides tools for rent collection, expense tracking, and tenant screening.

2. Standard Operating Procedures (SOPs)

Developing and implementing standard operating procedures (SOPs) can ensure consistency and efficiency in managing your properties. SOPs provide clear guidelines for handling various tasks and processes.

Key Areas for SOPs:

- Tenant Onboarding: Steps for screening, lease signing, and move-in processes.

- Rent Collection: Procedures for collecting rent, handling late payments, and issuing reminders.

- Maintenance Requests: Protocols for receiving, prioritizing, and addressing maintenance requests.

- Inspection and Upkeep: Regular inspection schedules and checklists for property upkeep.

- Tenant Communication: Guidelines for responding to tenant inquiries and resolving issues.

Benefits:

- Consistency: Ensures consistent handling of tasks and processes across properties.

- Efficiency: Streamlines operations, reducing time and effort required for management.

- Training: Provides a reference for training new staff or property managers.

Financial Management

1. Budgeting and Forecasting

Effective budgeting and forecasting are crucial for managing a larger portfolio. Develop comprehensive budgets that account for all income and expenses, and use forecasting to anticipate future financial needs.

Key Components:

- Income Projections: Estimate rental income based on current leases and occupancy rates.

- Expense Forecasting: Project property-related expenses, including maintenance, utilities, taxes, and management fees.

- Cash Flow Management: Monitor cash flow to ensure sufficient funds are available for ongoing expenses and unexpected repairs.

Tools:

- Spreadsheets: Use spreadsheets for detailed budgeting and forecasting.
- Software: Utilize property management software with financial management features for more sophisticated analysis.

2. Reserve Funds

Maintaining reserve funds provides financial security for unexpected expenses and capital improvements. Regularly contribute to these funds to build a financial cushion.

Types of Reserve Funds:

- Emergency Fund: Set aside funds for unexpected repairs and emergencies.
- Capital Improvement Fund: Save for long-term capital improvements, such as roof replacements or major renovations.

Strategies:

- Regular Contributions: Make regular contributions to reserve funds based on a percentage of rental income.
- Periodic Review: Review reserve fund levels periodically to ensure they are adequate for potential expenses.

3. Financial Reporting and Analysis

Regular financial reporting and analysis help you monitor the performance of your portfolio and make informed decisions. Generate and review key financial reports to assess profitability and identify areas for improvement.

Key Reports:

- Income Statement: Tracks revenue and expenses, showing net income or loss.

- Balance Sheet: Provides a snapshot of assets, liabilities, and equity.

- Cash Flow Statement: Tracks cash inflows and outflows to monitor liquidity.

Analysis Techniques:

- Ratio Analysis: Use financial ratios, such as the debt-to-equity ratio and cap rate, to assess financial health.

- Comparative Analysis: Compare performance across properties to identify trends and outliers.

Tenant Management

1. Tenant Relations

Maintaining positive tenant relations is essential for tenant retention and satisfaction. Implement effective communication and conflict resolution strategies to address tenant concerns and build strong relationships.

Key Strategies:

- Regular Communication: Keep tenants informed about property-related updates and changes.

- Prompt Response: Respond to tenant inquiries and maintenance requests promptly.

- Feedback Mechanism: Implement a system for collecting tenant feedback and addressing concerns.

2. Tenant Screening and Onboarding

Thorough tenant screening and effective onboarding processes are crucial for attracting and retaining high-quality tenants. Develop standardized procedures for tenant screening and onboarding.

Screening Process:

- Application Form: Collect comprehensive information through a detailed rental application form.

- Background Checks: Conduct credit, criminal, and rental history checks to assess tenant reliability.

- References: Verify employment and contact

previous landlords for references.

Onboarding Process:

- Lease Agreement: Ensure tenants fully understand and agree to lease terms.

- Move-In Inspection: Conduct a move-in inspection to document property condition.

- Orientation: Provide a property orientation to familiarize tenants with the property and procedures.

Maintenance and Repairs

1. Preventive Maintenance

Implementing preventive maintenance practices can help you identify and address issues before they become major problems. Regular inspections and maintenance can extend the life of your property and reduce long-term costs.

Key Practices:

- Scheduled Inspections: Conduct regular inspections of key systems, such as HVAC, plumbing, and electrical.

- Seasonal Maintenance: Perform seasonal maintenance tasks, such as winterizing plumbing and servicing heating systems.

- Documentation: Maintain detailed records of

all maintenance activities and inspections.

2. Vendor Management

Establishing strong relationships with reliable vendors and contractors is essential for efficient maintenance and repairs. Develop a network of trusted professionals to handle various maintenance tasks.

Key Strategies:

- Vendor Selection: Select vendors based on experience, reliability, and cost-effectiveness.

- Service Agreements: Establish service agreements with key vendors for regular maintenance and emergency repairs.

- Performance Monitoring: Monitor vendor performance and provide feedback to ensure high-quality service.

3. Emergency Preparedness

Having a plan in place for emergency situations can help you respond quickly and effectively to protect your properties and tenants.

Emergency Plan:

- Contact Information: Maintain up-to-date contact information for emergency services and key vendors.

- Communication Protocol: Establish a communication protocol for notifying tenants and coordinating responses.

- Resource Allocation: Ensure you have the necessary resources, such as emergency funds and supplies, to address emergencies.

Scaling your real estate portfolio requires strategic planning, leveraging equity, and implementing robust systems and processes. By understanding how to leverage the equity in your existing properties, you can finance new acquisitions and grow your portfolio. Effective management of a larger portfolio involves investing in property management software, developing standard operating procedures, and implementing strong financial and tenant management practices.

Maintaining a proactive approach to maintenance and repairs, establishing strong vendor relationships, and preparing for emergencies are also crucial for managing an expanding portfolio. By following these guidelines, you can achieve sustainable growth, maximize returns, and build a successful and diversified real estate portfolio.

Chapter 10:

Navigating Challenges

Navigating Challenges

Building and managing a successful real estate portfolio involves navigating various challenges that can arise from economic fluctuations, tenant turnover, and legal issues. This section will explore strategies for preparing for market downturns, minimizing vacancies, and handling legal challenges to ensure the long-term success and stability of your real estate investments.

Economic Downturns: Preparing for Market Fluctuations

Economic downturns can significantly impact real estate investments, affecting property values, rental income, and occupancy rates. Preparing for market fluctuations and implementing strategies to mitigate their impact is crucial for maintaining the stability and profitability of your portfolio.

1. Building a Financial Cushion

A strong financial cushion can help you weather economic downturns and maintain your investments during challenging times.

Emergency Fund:

- Purpose: Set aside an emergency fund to cover unexpected expenses, such as major repairs or vacancies, during economic downturns.

- Amount: Aim to save at least three to six months' worth of operating expenses for each property.

Reserve Fund:

- Capital Improvements: Establish a reserve fund for long-term capital improvements, such as roof replacements or HVAC upgrades, to avoid financial strain during downturns.

- Regular Contributions: Make regular contributions to the reserve fund based on rental income and projected expenses.

2. Diversifying Your Portfolio

Diversification is a key strategy for reducing risk and ensuring stability during economic downturns.

Property Types:

- Residential Properties: Invest in a mix of single-family homes, multi-family properties, and condos to spread risk and create multiple income streams.

- Commercial Properties: Consider investing in commercial properties, such as office buildings, retail spaces, and industrial properties, to further diversify your portfolio.

Geographic Locations:

- Local Markets: Invest in properties across different local markets to reduce the impact of regional economic fluctuations.

- National and International Markets: Explore investment opportunities in national and international markets to access diverse growth opportunities and minimize exposure to localized economic downturns.

3. Maintaining Strong Occupancy Rates

High occupancy rates are essential for maintaining rental income and financial stability during economic downturns.

Tenant Retention:

- Quality Tenants: Focus on attracting and retaining high-quality tenants by providing excellent customer service, maintaining the property, and addressing tenant concerns promptly.

- Lease Renewals: Encourage lease renewals by offering incentives, such as rent discounts or upgrades, to retain long-term tenants.

Marketing and Tenant Acquisition:

- Effective Marketing: Implement targeted marketing strategies to attract new tenants quickly and minimize vacancies.

- Screening Process: Develop a thorough tenant screening process to ensure you select reliable and responsible tenants.

4. Flexible Lease Terms

Offering flexible lease terms can help attract and retain tenants during economic downturns.

Short-Term Leases:

- Flexibility: Provide short-term lease options to accommodate tenants who may be uncertain about their long-term plans during economic fluctuations.

- Premium Pricing: Charge a premium for short-term leases to offset the potential risk of higher turnover.

Lease Adjustments:

- Negotiation: Be open to negotiating lease terms, such as rent adjustments or payment plans, to retain tenants facing financial difficulties.

- Renewal Incentives: Offer incentives for lease renewals, such as reduced rent increases or property upgrades, to encourage long-term tenancy.

5. Monitoring Economic Indicators

Staying informed about economic indicators and market trends can help you anticipate downturns and adjust your strategy accordingly.

Key Indicators:

- Employment Rates: Monitor local and national employment rates, as job stability directly impacts tenants' ability to pay rent.

- GDP Growth: Track GDP growth to gauge overall economic health and predict potential downturns.
- Inflation Rates: Keep an eye on inflation rates, as rising costs can affect both property expenses and tenants' financial stability.

Market Research:

- Regular Analysis: Conduct regular market research to stay informed about real estate trends, property values, and rental demand in your target markets.

- Professional Insights: Consult with real estate professionals, such as agents and analysts, to gain expert insights and recommendations.

Tenant Turnover: Minimizing Vacancies and Finding New Tenants

Tenant turnover can lead to vacancies, loss of rental income, and additional expenses for marketing and tenant acquisition. Implementing strategies to minimize vacancies and efficiently find new tenants is crucial for maintaining a profitable and stable portfolio.

1. Enhancing Tenant Retention

Focusing on tenant retention is one of the most effective ways to minimize turnover and maintain high occupancy rates.

Positive Tenant Experience:

- Communication: Maintain open and transparent communication with tenants to build trust and address concerns promptly.

- Responsive Maintenance: Provide timely and efficient maintenance services to ensure tenant satisfaction and property upkeep.

Incentives for Renewals:

- Rent Discounts: Offer rent discounts or limited rent increases to encourage lease renewals and long-term tenancy.

- Upgrades: Provide property upgrades, such as new appliances or cosmetic improvements, as incentives for renewing leases.

2. Efficient Turnover Management

Managing the turnover process efficiently can reduce the time a property remains vacant and minimize loss of rental income.

Pre-Move-Out Inspections:

- Advance Notice: Conduct pre-move-out inspections to identify any necessary repairs or maintenance tasks before the tenant vacates.

- Scheduling: Schedule repairs and cleaning services in advance to ensure a quick turnaround between tenants.

Streamlined Processes:

- Standardized Procedures: Develop standardized procedures for move-out inspections, cleaning, repairs, and marketing to streamline the turnover process.

- Vendor Relationships: Establish relationships with reliable vendors and contractors to ensure prompt and quality service during turnovers.

3. Effective Marketing Strategies

Implementing effective marketing strategies can help you attract new tenants quickly and minimize vacancies.

Online Listings:

- Visibility: List your properties on popular online rental platforms, such as Zillow, Trulia, and Craigslist, to reach a wide audience.

- High-Quality Photos: Use high-quality photos and detailed descriptions to showcase the property's features and amenities.

Social Media:

- Engagement: Utilize social media platforms, such as Facebook, Instagram, and Twitter, to promote your rental properties and engage with potential tenants.

- Targeted Ads: Run targeted advertising campaigns on social media to reach specific demographics and increase visibility.

Local Marketing:

- Signage: Use eye-catching "For Rent" signs on the property to attract local traffic and inquiries.

- Community Involvement: Participate in local community events and network with local businesses to promote your rental properties.

4. Thorough Tenant Screening

Conducting thorough tenant screening is essential for selecting reliable and responsible tenants, reducing the risk of future turnover.

Application Process:

- Comprehensive Applications: Collect detailed information through comprehensive rental applications, including employment history, income verification, and references.

- Background Checks: Conduct credit, criminal, and rental history checks to assess the applicant's reliability and suitability.

Interviewing:

- Personal Interaction: Conduct in-person or virtual interviews with prospective tenants to gauge their compatibility and address any questions or concerns.

- Verification: Verify employment and contact previous landlords to gather additional information about the applicant's rental history.

5. Competitive Rental Rates

Setting competitive rental rates can help attract and retain tenants, reducing the likelihood of vacancies.

Market Analysis:

- Comparable Properties: Conduct a market analysis to compare rental rates of similar properties in the area.

- Adjustments: Adjust rental rates based on market demand, property features, and location to remain competitive.

Flexible Pricing:

- Promotions: Offer promotional pricing or move-in incentives, such as reduced security deposits or first month's rent discounts, to attract new tenants.

- Negotiation: Be open to negotiating rental rates with prospective tenants to reach mutually beneficial agreements.

Legal Challenges: Staying Compliant and Handling Disputes

Navigating legal challenges is a critical aspect of property management. Staying compliant with local, state, and federal regulations and effectively handling disputes can protect your investments and maintain positive tenant relationships.

1. Understanding Landlord-Tenant Laws

Familiarity with landlord-tenant laws is essential for ensuring compliance and avoiding legal disputes.

Key Areas:

- Fair Housing Laws: Ensure compliance with fair housing laws that prohibit discrimination based on race, color, religion, sex, national origin, familial status, and disability.

- Security Deposits: Understand regulations regarding security deposit collection, handling, and return.

- Lease Agreements: Ensure lease agreements comply with local laws and clearly outline the rights and responsibilities of both parties.

Resources:

- Legal Counsel: Consult with a real estate attorney to stay informed about legal requirements and receive guidance on complex issues.

- Education: Attend workshops, seminars, and courses on landlord-tenant laws to stay updated on legal changes and best practices.

2. Drafting Comprehensive Lease Agreements

A comprehensive lease agreement is a critical tool for preventing disputes and ensuring clear communication of terms and conditions.

Key Components:

- Lease Terms: Clearly outline the lease term, rent amount, due dates, and payment methods.

- Maintenance Responsibilities: Specify the maintenance responsibilities of both the landlord and tenant.

- Rules and Regulations: Include property rules and regulations, such as noise policies, pet policies, and use of common areas.

- Dispute Resolution: Outline the process for resolving disputes, including mediation or arbitration clauses.

Custom Clauses:

- Custom Provisions: Include custom clauses tailored to the specific needs of the property and tenancy, such as clauses for property inspections or early termination.

3. Handling Tenant Disputes

Effectively handling tenant disputes can prevent escalation and maintain positive tenant relationships.

Communication:

- Open Dialogue: Encourage open communication with tenants to address concerns and resolve issues promptly.

- Documentation: Document all communications and actions taken to resolve disputes for future reference.

Mediation:

- Third-Party Mediation: Engage a neutral third-party mediator to facilitate discussions and help both parties reach a mutually agreeable solution when disputes arise.

Legal Action:

- Eviction Process: Understand the legal process for eviction and follow all required steps to ensure compliance with local laws.

- Legal Counsel: Consult with an attorney for guidance on handling disputes that may require legal action, such as lease violations or non-payment of rent.

4. Staying Updated on Legal Changes

Laws and regulations governing rental properties can change frequently. Staying updated on these changes is crucial for ensuring ongoing compliance.

Key Strategies:

- Regular Reviews: Conduct regular reviews of local, state, and federal laws to identify any changes that may impact your rental properties.

- Professional Associations: Join professional associations, such as the National Apartment Association (NAA) or the National Association of Residential Property Managers (NARPM), to access resources and stay informed about legal updates.

- Continuing Education: Participate in

continuing education courses and seminars on landlord-tenant law to stay current on best practices and legal requirements.

5. Implementing Compliance Programs

Implementing compliance programs can help ensure that your properties and management practices adhere to all applicable laws and regulations.

Compliance Audits:

- Regular Audits: Conduct regular compliance audits to review your properties and management practices for adherence to legal requirements.

- Action Plans: Develop action plans to address any compliance issues identified during audits.

Training Programs:

- Staff Training: Provide regular training for property managers and staff on legal requirements and best practices for compliance.

- Tenant Education: Educate tenants about their rights and responsibilities under the lease agreement and relevant laws.

Navigating challenges in real estate investing requires proactive strategies and a thorough understanding of market dynamics, tenant management, and legal compliance. By preparing for economic downturns, minimizing tenant turnover, and handling legal challenges effectively, you can maintain the stability and profitability of your real estate portfolio.

Preparing for Economic Downturns

Economic downturns are inevitable, but with careful planning and strategic measures, you can protect your investments and weather market fluctuations.

Building Financial Resilience:

- Establish a strong financial cushion with emergency and reserve funds to cover unexpected expenses and maintain stability during economic downturns.

- Diversify your portfolio across different property types and geographic locations to spread risk and reduce the impact of localized economic fluctuations.

Maintaining Occupancy Rates:

- Focus on tenant retention through positive tenant experiences, responsive maintenance, and incentives for lease renewals.

- Implement effective marketing strategies to attract new tenants quickly and minimize vacancies.

Monitoring Economic Indicators:

- Stay informed about key economic

indicators, such as employment rates, GDP growth, and inflation rates, to anticipate downturns and adjust your strategy accordingly.

Minimizing Tenant Turnover

Tenant turnover can be costly and disruptive, but with the right strategies, you can minimize vacancies and maintain a steady stream of rental income.

Enhancing Tenant Retention:

- Provide excellent customer service, maintain open communication, and respond promptly to tenant concerns to build positive relationships and encourage long-term tenancy.

- Offer incentives for lease renewals, such as rent discounts or property upgrades, to retain quality tenants.

Efficient Turnover Management:

- Streamline the turnover process with standardized procedures for move-out inspections, cleaning, repairs, and marketing to reduce vacancy periods.

- Establish relationships with reliable vendors and contractors to ensure prompt and quality service during turnovers.

Effective Marketing and Tenant Screening:

- Implement targeted marketing strategies to attract new tenants quickly, and conduct thorough tenant screening to select reliable and responsible tenants.

- Set competitive rental rates based on market analysis to attract and retain tenants.

Handling Legal Challenges

Navigating legal challenges is a critical aspect of property management. By staying compliant with laws and effectively handling disputes, you can protect your investments and maintain positive tenant relationships.

Understanding Landlord-Tenant Laws:

- Familiarize yourself with landlord-tenant laws at the local, state, and federal levels to ensure compliance and avoid legal disputes.

- Consult with legal counsel and participate in continuing education to stay updated on legal changes and best practices.

Drafting Comprehensive Lease Agreements:

- Develop comprehensive lease agreements that clearly outline terms and conditions, maintenance responsibilities, and rules and regulations to prevent disputes.

- Include custom clauses tailored to the specific needs of your properties and tenants.

Effective Dispute Resolution:

- Encourage open communication with tenants to address concerns and resolve issues promptly.

- Utilize mediation and legal counsel when necessary to handle disputes and ensure compliance with legal requirements.

Staying Updated and Implementing Compliance Programs:

- Conduct regular reviews of laws and regulations, participate in professional associations, and provide training for property managers and staff to stay updated on legal changes.

- Implement compliance programs with regular audits and action plans to ensure adherence to legal requirements.

By following these strategies and best practices, you can navigate the challenges of economic downturns, tenant turnover, and legal issues effectively. This will enable you to maintain a stable and profitable real estate portfolio, ensuring long-term success and growth.

Real estate investment can be highly rewarding but also comes with its share of challenges. Among the most significant are unexpected repairs and costs, as well as the need to adapt to ever-changing market conditions. This section will delve into strategies for building a financial cushion to handle unforeseen expenses and maintaining flexibility and awareness to stay ahead of market changes.

Unexpected Repairs and Costs: Building a Financial Cushion

Unexpected repairs and maintenance costs are an inevitable part of property management. Whether it's a sudden plumbing issue, a roof that needs replacement, or an HVAC system failure, these costs can strain your finances if you're not prepared. Building a financial cushion is crucial to ensure you can handle these surprises without jeopardizing your investment.

1. Understanding Common Unexpected Repairs

Plumbing Issues:

- Common Problems: Burst pipes, leaks, clogged drains, and faulty water heaters are common plumbing issues that can cause significant damage if not addressed promptly.

- Prevention and Maintenance: Regular inspections and maintenance, such as checking for leaks and servicing water heaters, can help prevent major issues.

Electrical Problems:

- Common Problems: Faulty wiring, circuit overloads, and outdated electrical systems can pose safety hazards and require immediate attention.

- Prevention and Maintenance: Ensure regular inspections and updates to electrical systems to meet current safety standards.

Structural Repairs:

- Common Problems: Foundation cracks, roof leaks, and structural damage can be costly and complex to repair.

- Prevention and Maintenance: Regular property inspections and timely repairs of minor issues can prevent larger structural problems.

HVAC System Failures:

- Common Problems: Air conditioning or heating system failures can be inconvenient for tenants and expensive to fix.

- Prevention and Maintenance: Schedule regular HVAC maintenance, including filter replacements and system checks, to ensure efficient operation.

2. Building an Emergency Fund

An emergency fund is essential for covering

unexpected repairs and maintenance costs without disrupting your cash flow.

Determining Fund Size:

- Monthly Expenses: Calculate the average monthly operating expenses for each property, including mortgage payments, utilities, insurance, and maintenance costs.

- Fund Amount: Aim to save three to six months' worth of operating expenses for each property to cover unexpected repairs and vacancies.

Setting Up the Fund:

- Separate Account: Open a separate savings account specifically for the emergency fund to keep it distinct from other funds.

- Regular Contributions: Make regular contributions to the emergency fund, setting aside a portion of rental income each month.

3. Establishing a Reserve Fund

In addition to an emergency fund, a reserve fund is necessary for long-term capital improvements and major repairs.

Purpose of Reserve Fund:

- Capital Improvements: Use the reserve fund for significant capital improvements, such as roof replacements, plumbing upgrades, and major renovations.

- Unexpected Major Repairs: Cover unexpected major repairs that exceed the capacity of the emergency fund.

Determining Fund Size:

- Property Age and Condition: Consider the age and condition of your properties when determining the reserve fund size, as older properties may require more substantial repairs.

- Projected Costs: Estimate the costs of major repairs and improvements over the next five to ten years and plan the reserve fund accordingly.

Setting Up the Fund:

- Separate Account: Open a dedicated account for the reserve fund to keep it separate from other funds.

- Regular Contributions: Contribute regularly to the reserve fund, adjusting the amount based on rental income and projected expenses.

4. Budgeting for Ongoing Maintenance

Regular maintenance is crucial to preventing unexpected repairs and extending the lifespan of your property.

Annual Maintenance Budget:

- Estimate Costs: Estimate annual maintenance costs based on historical expenses and industry standards (typically 1-3% of the property's value).

- Allocate Funds: Allocate a portion of the rental income each month to the annual maintenance budget.

Scheduled Maintenance:

- Seasonal Tasks: Schedule seasonal maintenance tasks, such as HVAC servicing, gutter cleaning, and landscaping, to keep the property in good condition.

- Routine Inspections: Conduct routine inspections to identify and address minor issues before they become major problems.

5. Insurance and Warranties

Insurance and warranties can provide additional financial protection against unexpected repairs and costs.

Property Insurance:

- Coverage: Ensure your property insurance policy covers common risks, such as fire, water damage, and natural disasters.

- Review Annually: Review your policy annually

to ensure it provides adequate coverage for your property's current value and condition.

Home Warranties:

- Coverage: Consider purchasing home warranties that cover major systems and appliances, such as HVAC, plumbing, and electrical systems.

- Cost-Benefit Analysis: Conduct a cost-benefit analysis to determine if the warranty's coverage justifies the annual premium.

Adapting to Market Changes: Staying Flexible and Informed

The real estate market is dynamic, influenced by various economic, social, and political factors. Staying flexible and informed is essential to navigate these changes successfully and ensure the long-term profitability of your investments.

1. Understanding Market Trends

Economic Indicators:

- Employment Rates: Monitor employment rates, as job stability affects tenants' ability to pay rent and overall rental demand.

- Interest Rates: Track changes in interest rates, which can impact mortgage rates, property values, and investor demand.

- Inflation: Keep an eye on inflation rates, as rising costs can affect both property expenses and tenants' financial stability.

Real Estate Metrics:

- Occupancy Rates: Analyze occupancy rates in your target markets to assess rental demand and competition.

- Rental Rates: Monitor rental rate trends to ensure your properties are competitively priced and adjust rents accordingly.

- Property Values: Track changes in property values to assess the appreciation potential and equity growth of your investments.

Demographic Shifts:

- Population Growth: Identify areas with strong population growth, as these markets often have higher rental demand and property value appreciation.

- Migration Patterns: Monitor migration patterns to understand where people are moving and why, which can inform investment decisions.

2. Flexibility in Investment Strategy

Adapting your investment strategy to market changes can help you capitalize on new opportunities and mitigate risks.

Diversification:

- Property Types: Diversify your portfolio by investing in different types of properties, such as residential, commercial, and industrial, to spread risk and increase income streams.

- Geographic Locations: Invest in multiple geographic locations to reduce exposure to regional economic fluctuations and access diverse growth opportunities.

Market Entry and Exit:

- Entry Timing: Be flexible with your market entry timing, buying properties when prices are favorable and demand is high.

- Exit Strategy: Develop a clear exit strategy for each investment, including criteria for selling or refinancing based on market conditions and investment goals.

Value-Add Opportunities:

- Renovations: Identify properties with value-add opportunities, such as those requiring renovations or updates, to increase rental income and property value.

- Repositioning: Consider repositioning strategies, such as converting underperforming properties to higher-demand uses (e.g., office to residential), to maximize returns.

3. Leveraging Technology

Utilizing technology can enhance your ability to adapt to market changes and manage your portfolio efficiently.

Property Management Software:

- Automation: Automate routine tasks, such as rent collection, maintenance requests, and tenant communication, to streamline operations and reduce manual work.

- Data Analytics: Use data analytics tools to track key performance metrics, analyze market trends, and make data-driven investment decisions.

Market Research Tools:

- Online Platforms: Leverage online platforms and databases, such as Zillow, Redfin, and CoStar, to access real-time market data and property information.

- Research Reports: Subscribe to industry research reports and newsletters to stay informed about market trends, forecasts, and emerging opportunities.

Virtual Tours and Marketing:

- Virtual Tours: Utilize virtual tour technology to showcase properties to potential tenants and buyers, especially in remote or competitive markets.

- Digital Marketing: Implement digital marketing strategies, such as social media advertising and search engine optimization (SEO), to reach a broader audience and attract quality tenants.

4. Continuous Learning and Networking

Staying informed and connected within the real estate industry is crucial for adapting to market changes and accessing new opportunities.

Education:

- Courses and Workshops: Participate in real estate courses, workshops, and seminars to enhance your knowledge and skills in areas such as property management, investment analysis, and legal compliance.

- Certifications: Consider obtaining relevant certifications, such as Certified Property Manager (CPM) or Certified Commercial Investment Member (CCIM), to demonstrate expertise and credibility.

Networking:

- Industry Associations: Join industry associations, such as the National Association of Realtors (NAR) and the Urban Land Institute (ULI), to access resources, events, and networking opportunities.

- Local Groups: Participate in local real estate investment groups and meetups to connect with other investors, share insights, and collaborate on projects.

Mentorship:

- Mentors: Seek mentorship from experienced real estate investors and professionals who can provide guidance, advice, and support as you navigate market changes.

- Peer Learning: Engage in peer learning through mastermind groups or online forums to exchange ideas, challenges, and solutions with fellow investors.

5. Scenario Planning and Risk Management

Developing scenario plans and risk management strategies can help you anticipate and respond to market changes effectively.

Scenario Planning:

- Best-Case Scenario: Plan for the best-case scenario, where market conditions are favorable, and your investments perform exceptionally well.

- Worst-Case Scenario: Prepare for the worst-case scenario, where market downturns or unexpected events significantly impact your investments.

- Moderate Scenario: Consider a moderate scenario, where market conditions fluctuate but remain relatively stable.

Risk Management Strategies:

- Contingency Plans: Develop contingency plans for different scenarios, outlining specific actions to take in response to market changes.

- Insurance: Ensure you have adequate insurance coverage for your properties, including property insurance, liability insurance, and loss of rental income coverage.

- Financial Buffers: Maintain financial buffers, such as emergency and reserve funds, to provide a cushion against unexpected expenses and market downturns.

Navigating challenges in real estate investment requires proactive planning, financial preparedness, and adaptability. By building a financial cushion to handle unexpected repairs and costs, you can protect your investments and maintain stability during unforeseen events. Staying flexible and informed allows you to adapt to market changes, capitalize on new opportunities, and mitigate risks.

Building a Financial Cushion:

- Establish emergency and reserve funds to cover unexpected repairs, maintenance costs, and long-term capital improvements.

- Budget for ongoing maintenance and utilize insurance and warranties to provide additional financial protection.

Adapting to Market Changes:

- Understand market trends and economic indicators to anticipate changes and adjust your strategy accordingly.

- Maintain flexibility in your investment strategy, leveraging technology, continuous learning, and networking to stay informed and connected.

- Develop scenario plans and risk management strategies to prepare for different market conditions and ensure long-term success.

By following these strategies and best practices, you can navigate the challenges of real estate investment effectively, ensuring the stability and profitability of your portfolio.

Chapter 11:

Long-term Success and Exit Strategies

Long-term Success and Exit Strategies

Achieving long-term success in real estate investment requires a well-thought-out approach that encompasses building wealth over time, reinvestment strategies, exit strategies, legacy planning, and continuous learning. This comprehensive section explores these critical elements in detail, providing actionable insights to help you sustain and grow your real estate portfolio effectively.

Building Wealth Over Time: Compounding Returns and Reinvestment

Building wealth through real estate involves leveraging the power of compounding returns and strategic reinvestment. Understanding these concepts and how to apply them can significantly enhance your long-term financial growth.

1. Understanding Compounding Returns

Concept of Compounding:

- Definition: Compounding refers to the process where the returns on an investment generate additional returns over time, leading to exponential growth.

- Impact: In real estate, compounding can occur through appreciation, rental income reinvestment, and mortgage principal reduction.

Real Estate Examples:

- Appreciation: As property values increase, the equity in your investment grows, creating more wealth.

- Rental Income: Reinvesting rental income into additional properties or paying down existing mortgages accelerates wealth accumulation.

- Mortgage Reduction: Regular mortgage payments reduce the principal balance, increasing equity and leveraging potential.

Illustration:

- Scenario: You purchase a property for $200,000 with a 20% down payment. Over ten years, the property appreciates by 3% annually, and you reinvest the rental income.

- Results: After ten years, the property's value increases to approximately $268,783, and reinvested rental income further enhances your portfolio's growth.

2. Strategic Reinvestment

Reinvestment Options:

- Additional Properties: Use rental income and profits from existing properties to acquire new investments.

- Property Improvements: Invest in renovations and upgrades to increase property value and rental income potential.

- Debt Reduction: Accelerate mortgage payments to build equity faster and reduce interest costs.

Benefits of Reinvestment:

- Portfolio Growth: Reinvestment enables you to acquire more properties, increasing your overall wealth and income potential.

- Increased Cash Flow: Improvements and debt reduction can enhance rental income and reduce expenses, boosting cash flow.

- Risk Mitigation: Diversifying investments through reinvestment reduces risk by spreading it across multiple properties.

Example:

- Scenario: You own a rental property generating $1,500 monthly in net income. By reinvesting this income into another property, you can double your portfolio's value and income potential over time.

Reinvestment Strategies: Growing Your Portfolio Strategic reinvestment is essential for scaling your real estate portfolio and maximizing returns. This section explores various reinvestment strategies to help you grow your portfolio effectively.

1. Acquiring Additional Properties

Identifying Opportunities:

- Market Research: Conduct thorough market research to identify high-growth areas and undervalued properties.

- Networking: Leverage your network of real estate professionals to uncover off-market deals and investment opportunities.

Financing Options:

- Leveraging Equity: Use the equity in existing properties to finance new acquisitions through cash-out refinancing, home equity loans, or HELOCs.

- Traditional Mortgages: Secure traditional mortgages for new purchases, considering interest rates, loan terms, and down payment requirements.

- Private Financing: Explore private financing options, such as partnerships or joint ventures, to access additional capital.

Risk Management:

- Diversification: Diversify your portfolio by investing in different property types and locations to spread risk.

- Due Diligence: Perform thorough due diligence on potential acquisitions, including property inspections, market analysis, and financial projections.

2. Property Improvements and Value-Add Strategies

Renovations and Upgrades:

- Interior Improvements: Focus on high-impact renovations, such as kitchen and bathroom upgrades, flooring, and painting, to increase property value and rental appeal.

- Exterior Enhancements: Improve curb appeal with landscaping, exterior painting, and roof repairs to attract quality tenants and increase property value.

Value-Add Opportunities:

- Repositioning: Reposition underperforming properties by changing their use or target market, such as converting commercial spaces to residential units.

- Increasing Rent: Implement strategic rent

increases based on market demand and property improvements to enhance rental income.

Financing Improvements:

- Renovation Loans: Secure renovation loans or use HELOCs to finance property improvements without depleting cash reserves.

- Cash Flow Reinvestment: Reinvest rental income into property improvements to enhance value and income potential.

3. Leveraging Technology and Automation

Property Management Software:

- Efficiency: Use property management software to streamline operations, automate rent collection, and manage maintenance requests.

- Data Analytics: Leverage data analytics to track performance metrics, identify trends, and make informed investment decisions.

Digital Marketing:

- Online Listings: Utilize online platforms and social media to market properties, attract tenants, and reduce vacancies.

- Virtual Tours: Implement virtual tours to showcase properties to potential tenants and buyers, especially in remote or competitive markets.

Smart Home Technology:

- Tenant Attraction: Invest in smart home technology, such as keyless entry, smart thermostats, and security systems, to attract tech-savvy tenants and increase rental value.

- Efficiency: Use smart technology to monitor and manage energy usage, reducing utility costs and improving property efficiency.

Exit Strategies: Knowing When and How to Sell

An effective exit strategy is crucial for maximizing returns and achieving long-term investment goals. Understanding when and how to sell properties can significantly impact your financial success.

1. Timing the Market

Market Conditions:

- Seller's Market: Sell properties in a seller's market, where demand is high, and supply is low, to maximize sale prices and returns.

- Economic Indicators: Monitor economic indicators, such as interest rates, employment rates, and GDP growth, to identify favorable selling conditions.

Property Performance:

- Appreciation: Consider selling properties that have significantly appreciated in value to realize gains and reinvest in new opportunities.

- Cash Flow: Evaluate properties with declining cash flow or increasing maintenance costs and consider selling to optimize portfolio performance.

2. Preparing for Sale

Property Assessment:

- Valuation: Obtain a professional appraisal to determine the property's market value and set a competitive asking price.

- Condition: Assess the property's condition and make necessary repairs and improvements to enhance its appeal and value.

Marketing Strategy:

- Professional Photography: Use high-quality photos and virtual tours to showcase the property's features and attract potential buyers.

- Online Listings: List the property on popular real estate platforms and leverage social media and digital marketing to reach a wide audience.

Working with Professionals:

- Real Estate Agents: Partner with experienced real estate agents to navigate the selling process, negotiate offers, and secure the best possible sale price.

- Legal and Financial Advisors: Consult with legal and financial advisors to ensure a smooth transaction and address any legal or tax implications.

3. Strategic Selling

Partial Liquidation:

- Diversification: Consider selling a portion of your portfolio to diversify investments and reduce risk.

- Reinvestment: Reinvest proceeds from the sale into new properties or other investment opportunities to continue growing your wealth.

1031 Exchange:

- Tax Deferral: Utilize a 1031 exchange to defer capital gains taxes by reinvesting proceeds from the sale into a like-kind property.

- Reinvestment Opportunities: Identify new investment opportunities that align with your long-term goals and growth strategy.

Exit Timing:

- Personal Goals: Align your exit strategy with personal financial goals, such as retirement planning, debt reduction, or funding major expenses.

- Market Conditions: Be flexible with exit timing, considering market conditions and potential future appreciation to maximize returns.

Legacy Planning: Passing on Your Real Estate Empire

Legacy planning ensures that your real estate investments benefit future generations and align with your long-term goals. Developing a comprehensive legacy plan can provide financial security for your heirs and preserve your wealth.

1. Estate Planning

Wills and Trusts:

- Will: Draft a will to specify how your real estate assets will be distributed to heirs and beneficiaries.

- Trust: Consider establishing a trust to manage and distribute assets according to your wishes, reduce estate taxes, and avoid probate.

Beneficiary Designations:

- Ownership Structures: Ensure beneficiary

designations are up to date and reflect your intentions for property distribution.

- Joint Ownership: Explore joint ownership options, such as joint tenancy with right of survivorship, to facilitate a smooth transfer of ownership.

Professional Advisors:

- Estate Planning Attorney: Work with an estate planning attorney to draft legal documents and navigate complex estate planning issues.

- Financial Advisor: Consult with a financial advisor to develop a comprehensive estate plan that aligns with your financial goals and minimizes tax liabilities.

2. Succession Planning

Family Involvement:

- Education and Training: Educate and train family members about real estate investment, property management, and financial planning to prepare them for future responsibilities.

- Roles and Responsibilities: Clearly define roles and responsibilities for family members involved in managing the real estate portfolio.

Business Structures:

- Family Trust: Establish a family trust to

manage and control real estate assets, ensuring a seamless transition to the next generation.

- Family Limited Partnership (FLP): Consider forming an FLP to transfer ownership interests to heirs while maintaining control and minimizing estate taxes.

Communication:

- Family Meetings: Hold regular family meetings to discuss the estate plan, address concerns, and ensure alignment with long-term goals.

- Transparency: Maintain open and transparent communication with heirs about your intentions, expectations, and the importance of preserving the real estate portfolio.

3. Philanthropic Goals

Charitable Giving:

- Donations: Consider donating real estate assets to charitable organizations or establishing a charitable trust to support causes that align with your values.

- Tax Benefits: Explore tax benefits associated with charitable giving, such as income tax deductions and estate tax reductions.

Legacy Projects:

- Community Impact: Invest in legacy projects that positively impact communities, such as affordable housing developments or community centers.

- Family Involvement: Involve family members in philanthropic initiatives to instill a sense of purpose and responsibility.

Continuous Learning and Improvement: Staying

Ahead in Real Estate

Continuous learning and improvement are essential for staying ahead in the competitive real estate market. Adopting a growth mindset and staying informed about industry trends can help you make better investment decisions and enhance your portfolio's performance.

1. Ongoing Education

Real Estate Courses:

- Formal Education: Enroll in real estate courses offered by universities, colleges, or online platforms to deepen your knowledge and skills.

- Certifications: Obtain relevant certifications, such as Certified Property Manager (CPM) or Certified Commercial Investment Member (CCIM), to demonstrate expertise and credibility.

- Workshops and Seminars:

- Industry Events: Attend workshops, seminars, and conferences to stay updated on industry trends, network with professionals, and gain insights from experts.

- Continuing Education: Participate in continuing education programs to keep your skills and knowledge current.

2. Staying Informed

Market Research:

- Data Sources: Utilize reputable data sources, such as government reports, industry publications, and market research firms, to access real-time market information.

- Trend Analysis: Analyze market trends, such as rental rates, occupancy levels, and property values, to inform investment decisions.

Professional Associations:

- Membership: Join professional associations, such as the National Association of Realtors (NAR) and the Urban Land Institute (ULI), to access resources, events, and networking opportunities.

- Publications: Subscribe to industry

publications and newsletters to stay informed about market developments, regulatory changes, and best practices.

3. Networking and Mentorship

Building Relationships:

- Industry Professionals: Network with real estate agents, brokers, property managers, lenders, and other industry professionals to build valuable relationships and gain insights.

- Investor Groups: Join real estate investor groups and associations to connect with like-minded individuals, share experiences, and collaborate on projects.

Mentorship:

- Finding a Mentor: Seek mentorship from experienced real estate investors and professionals who can provide guidance, advice, and support as you navigate the market.

- Mentorship Programs: Participate in formal mentorship programs offered by industry associations or educational institutions to gain structured mentorship and learning opportunities.

4. Technology and Innovation

Adopting New Technologies:

- Property Management Software: Invest in property management software to streamline operations, automate tasks, and enhance efficiency.

- Data Analytics: Leverage data analytics tools to track performance metrics, analyze market trends, and make data-driven investment decisions.

Staying Updated:

- Tech Trends: Stay updated on the latest technology trends and innovations in the real estate industry, such as virtual tours, smart home technology, and blockchain.

- Continuous Improvement: Continuously evaluate and adopt new technologies that can improve your investment strategy, property management, and overall portfolio performance.

Achieving long-term success in real estate investment involves building wealth over time through compounding returns and strategic reinvestment, growing your portfolio with effective reinvestment strategies, and developing well-defined exit strategies. Legacy planning ensures that your real estate investments benefit future generations, while continuous learning and improvement keep you ahead in the competitive real estate market.

Building Wealth Over Time:

- Leverage the power of compounding returns and strategic reinvestment to grow your wealth and enhance your portfolio's performance.

- Utilize various reinvestment strategies, such as acquiring additional properties, implementing value-add opportunities, and leveraging technology to maximize returns.

Exit Strategies:

- Develop effective exit strategies by timing the market, preparing properties for sale, and utilizing tax-efficient methods like 1031 exchanges.

- Align your exit strategy with personal financial goals and market conditions to optimize returns.

Legacy Planning:

- Ensure your real estate investments benefit future generations through comprehensive estate planning, succession planning, and philanthropic initiatives.

- Involve family members in the planning process and provide education and training to prepare them for future responsibilities.

Continuous Learning and Improvement:

- Stay ahead in the real estate market by pursuing ongoing education, staying informed about market trends, and building valuable relationships.

- Embrace new technologies and innovations to enhance your investment strategy and portfolio performance.

By following these strategies and best practices, you can achieve long-term success, sustain and grow your real estate portfolio, and create a lasting legacy for future generations.

www.ingramcontent.com/pod-product-compliance
Lightning Source LLC
Chambersburg PA
CBHW071910210526
45479CB00002B/354